THE
VEGGIE
CHRISTMAS
COOKBOOK

HarperCollins*Publishers*
1 London Bridge Street
London SE1 9GF

www.harpercollins.co.uk

First published by HarperCollins*Publishers* 2022

10 9 8 7 6 5 4 3 2 1

© HarperCollins*Publishers* 2022

Photographer: Joff Lee
Food Stylist: Mari Williams
Prop Stylist: Jo Harris/Topham Street

Heather Thomas asserts the moral right to be identified as the author of this work

A catalogue record of this book is available from the British Library

HB ISBN 978-0-00-855117-9
EB ISBN 978-0-00-855118-6

Printed and bound in Latvia

When using kitchen appliances please always follow the manufacturer's instructions.

MIX
Paper from
responsible sources
FSC™ C007454

FSC
www.fsc.org

This book is produced from independently certified FSC™ paper
to ensure responsible forest management.

For more information visit: www.harpercollins.co.uk/green

THE
VEGGIE
CHRISTMAS
COOKBOOK

HEATHER THOMAS

HarperCollins*Publishers*

CONTENTS

//

INTRODUCTION

Welcome to a delicious meat-free Christmas! It's now easier than ever before to get inspired and to create impressive vegetarian and plant-based vegan feasts. Nut roasts are off the menu as they are often the only option given to veggie guests. Instead, we have plenty of new festive favourites, plus the seasonal touches and trimmings that define Christmas food.

Being vegetarian or vegan doesn't mean you have to settle for second best during the Christmas holiday. This book shows you how to make special and joyful dishes with a sense of occasion that will delight and impress. We have spectacular desserts, traditional Christmas cakes, mince pies and teatime treats, as well as five-star dishes for the main event on Christmas Day.

At this time of year when you're craving comfort food and midwinter ingredients and flavours, we've taken the best of what's in season to create some showstopping meals that are simple to make or can be prepped and cooked ahead of time. This is the ultimate vegetarian and vegan cookbook for Christmas – perfect for parties and festive gatherings or intimate family get-togethers.

Christmas cooking and entertaining are less daunting when you plan ahead and shop, prep, cook and store or freeze some meals and party food well in advance. That way, you'll have more time to relax and enjoy spending it with your family and friends.

1. Make soups, stews and casseroles in advance and freeze them for easy no-fuss meals.

2. Make stuffing, gravies and sauces ahead of time and pop them in the freezer.

3. Some vegetable side dishes and even Yorkshire puddings freeze and reheat successfully.

4. Make the traditional Christmas cake up to 3 months beforehand and feed it with alcohol once every couple of weeks before icing.

5. Bake the mince pies the week before and store them in airtight containers.

6. Lebkuchen and shortbread can be made ahead and prettily wrapped as edible gifts.

THE CHRISTMAS STORE CUPBOARD

Make a shopping list and get stocked up ready for Christmas to avoid last-minute trips to the supermarket and deli. Here are some of the seasonal items you might find useful to keep in your store cupboard, fridge and freezer.

KITCHEN CUPBOARDS
· Vacuum-packed chestnuts
· Chutneys and pickles
· Bottled roasted red (bell) peppers in oil
· Tinned tomatoes and tomato purée (paste)
· Olive, nut, seed and vegetable oils
· Condiments: mustard, horseradish, sea salt flakes
· Ground and whole spices
· Dried herbs
· Seeds
· Curry paste
· Pesto sauce
· Cranberry sauce
· Nuts and nut butter
· Mincemeat
· Dried fruit and candied peel
· Vanilla extract
· Dark (bittersweet) chocolate (70% cocoa solids)
· Honey and maple syrup
· Coconut milk and cream
· Agar agar powder
· White, brown and icing (confectioner's) sugar
· Vegan-friendly fondant icing
· Rice, grains (quinoa, couscous, bulghur wheat) and pasta
· Lentils and beans
· Tinned chickpeas (garbanzos) for aquafaba
· Vegetable stock (bouillon) cubes
· Fresh fruit and vegetables

FRIDGE
· Tofu
· Seitan
· Shortcrust pastry, puff pastry and filo (phyllo) pastry (regular or vegan)
· Butter and vegan butter
· Cheese, e.g. Cheddar, Stilton, feta, mozzarella
· Vegan 'cheese' alternatives
· Eggs
· Vegetable stock
· Salad dressings
· Cream and dairy-free cream
· Milk and plant-based milk
· Yoghurt and plant-based yoghurt
· Fresh fruit, vegetables and salad leaves

FREEZER
· Bread, pizza bases, wraps and pita breads
· Mini Yorkshire puddings
· Ice cream and sorbets
· Frozen peas and vegetables
· Frozen gravy, sauces and stuffing
· Ice cubes

PARTIES AND ENTERTAINING

We have some great recipes for hot and cold party canapés, many of which can double as first-course appetizers when you're entertaining. If you are cooking a big Christmas lunch or dinner or a Boxing Day feast for family and friends, you'll find lots of festive ideas, including some fabulous savoury 'wreaths', 'crackers' and 'parcels', which taste as good as they look. Take it easy on yourself and make the festival less stressful with careful planning and prepping.

NOTHING GETS WASTED

We even have a section dedicated to using up Christmas leftovers in some innovative recipes for Boxing Day brunches, lunches, suppers and snacks. 'Recycle' your leftovers into sandwiches, wraps, stir-fries, risotto, curries, soups, pies and pasta bakes.

If you have leftover uncooked sprouts, even the tall stalks with the attached sprout rosettes can be used as attractive green columns to decorate your home, or you can remove the sprouts to make a seasonal wreath, interwoven with evergreens, holly and mistletoe – sustainable and aesthetically beautiful.

CHRISTMASSY
CANAPÉS

FESTIVE VIETNAMESE SPRING ROLLS

//

These delicious fresh spring rolls make a festive party dish with their colourful red, white and green filling. Serve them with a bowl of peanut sauce (below) or bottled sweet chilli sauce for dipping. You can buy rice paper wrappers in oriental stores, delis and large supermarkets.

MAKES 12
PREP 25 MINUTES

85g (3oz/¾ cup) shredded greens
1 large red (bell) pepper, deseeded and cut into thin strips
1 large carrot, cut into thin matchsticks (or grated)
50g (2oz/½ cup) bean sprouts
¼ cucumber, cut into thin matchsticks
a small handful of coriander (cilantro), chopped
2 tbsp light soy sauce
a squeeze of lime juice (optional)
12 round rice paper wrappers

PEANUT SAUCE
85g (3oz/⅓ cup) peanut butter
2 garlic cloves, crushed
3 tbsp fresh lime juice
2 tbsp soy sauce
1 tbsp toasted sesame oil
1–2 tbsp water

Make the peanut dipping sauce: whisk the peanut butter, garlic, lime juice, soy sauce and sesame oil in a bowl until well combined. Add the water, a tablespoon at a time, until smooth and creamy. Set aside while you make the spring rolls.

Put all the prepared vegetables in a bowl with the coriander, soy sauce and lime juice (if using) and toss lightly.

Fill a bowl with cold water and position it near you while you assemble the spring rolls.

Submerge a rice paper wrapper in the water for 5 seconds, or until pliable. Lay it out flat on a clean work surface and add some of the mixed vegetables, leaving a broad edge around them.

Fold the nearest end of the wrapper over the filling and then fold in the sides. Roll up like a parcel from the bottom to make a spring roll, finishing with the join underneath. Repeat with the rest of the wrappers and the vegetable filling.

Serve the spring rolls with the bowl of peanut sauce for dipping.

VARIATIONS
- Add a ripe mango, peeled, stoned (pitted) and cut into strips.
- Add peeled and grated radishes or mooli (daikon) or even some diced avocado.
- Add some grated fresh root ginger.

PARTY SAMOSAS

//

These Indian-spiced samosas taste delicious served hot or cold. They are traditionally fried but baking them in the oven is healthier. Serve them as canapés with a dash of chutney or with hot sauce for dipping.

MAKES 24
PREP 30 MINUTES
COOK 35–40 MINUTES

400g (14oz) sweet potatoes, peeled and diced
1 tbsp sunflower oil, plus extra for brushing
a bunch of spring onions (scallions), thinly sliced
2 garlic cloves, crushed
1 red chilli, deseeded and diced
1 tsp grated fresh root ginger
2 tsp black mustard seeds
1 tsp ground cumin
1 tsp ground turmeric
1 tbsp vegan curry paste
250g (9oz) spinach, washed, trimmed and shredded
a squeeze of lime juice
4 sheets of vegan filo (phyllo) pastry
sea salt and freshly ground black pepper
lime or mango chutney, to serve

VARIATIONS
· Substitute frozen peas for the spinach.
· Add a little coconut cream.

Preheat the oven to 200°C (180°C fan)/400°F/gas 6. Line a baking tray with baking parchment.

Cook the sweet potatoes in a pan of boiling water or a steamer for 8–10 minutes, or until just tender – they should still be a little firm and keep their shape. Drain well.

Meanwhile, heat the oil in a saucepan set over a low heat and cook the spring onions and garlic, stirring occasionally, for 2–3 minutes until softened. Add the chilli, ginger, seeds and ground spices and cook for 2 minutes. Stir in the curry paste and cook for 1 minute.

Stir in the spinach leaves and cook for 2–3 minutes until they wilt into the mixture. Gently stir in the sweet potato and lime juice. Check the seasoning, adding salt and pepper if needed, and leave to cool.

Place one sheet of filo pastry on a clean work surface and cut in half horizontally. Cut each half sheet lengthways into three strips, so you end up with 6 long strips.

Put a spoonful of the cooled sweet potato mixture in the top right-hand corner of each strip of pastry. Fold the pastry over the filling at an angle to make a triangle, then keep on folding it over until you get to the bottom of each strip. You should end up with a neat triangular parcel enclosing the filling. Repeat with the remaining sheets of filo pastry and the sweet potato mixture to make 24 samosas.

Brush the samosas lightly with oil and place on the lined baking tray. Cook in the preheated oven for 25 minutes, or until crisp and golden. Serve warm or cold with lime or mango chutney.

VEGAN HALLOUMI FRIES

//

You can buy blocks of plant-based halloumi cheese in most wholefood stores and some supermarkets. It has a similar texture to regular dairy halloumi and can be fried in the same way until crispy on the outside but melting inside. Serve these crispy fries with a selection of vegan dips, such as hummus and dairy-free tzatziki or even spicy fresh salsa or guacamole.

SERVES 6-8
PREP 10 MINUTES
COOK 4 MINUTES

150g (5oz/1 cup) rice flour
½ tsp sea salt
1 tsp ground cumin
1 tsp dried oregano
½ tsp grated lemon zest
400g (14oz) plant-based halloumi
120ml (4fl oz/½ cup) olive oil
smoked paprika, for dusting
freshly ground black pepper
vegan dips, to serve

Mix together the flour, salt, cumin, oregano, lemon zest and a grinding of black pepper in a bowl.

Slice the halloumi lengthways into fingers and dip each one quickly into a small bowl of cold water and then into the flour mixture so that it is well coated.

Heat the oil in a large frying pan (skillet) set over a medium heat. When it's hot, add the halloumi and fry for 2 minutes on each side, or until crispy and golden brown. Remove from the pan and drain on kitchen paper (paper towels).

Serve the halloumi fries immediately while they're piping hot, dusted with paprika and with some dips (see intro above).

VARIATIONS
· Sprinkle the fries with za'atar and chopped mint
· Drizzle the fries with hot sauce, e.g. sriracha.
· Serve with a bowl of dairy-free yoghurt swirled with chilli sauce or harissa.
· Serve the halloumi fries souvlaki-style, wrapped in a warm pita bread with salad.

CHRISTMAS FILO 'CRACKERS'

//

These little crispy 'crackers' are filled with a delicious mixture of melting cheese and sweet cranberry sauce. They are easy to assemble and are the perfect canapés at a Christmas drinks or buffet party. You could also serve them as an appetizer.

MAKES 42
PREP 30 MINUTES
COOK 10 MINUTES

85g (3oz/scant ½ cup) unsalted butter
7 sheets of filo (phyllo) pastry
300g (10oz) Brie, cut into 42 thin strips
300g (10oz/1 cup) cranberry sauce
30g (1oz/¼ cup) toasted pine nuts
white sesame seeds, for sprinkling
a bunch of chives, for tying (optional)

Preheat the oven to 200°C (180°C fan)/400°F/gas 6. Line 2 baking trays with baking parchment.

Place the butter in a pan set over a low heat and as soon as it melts, remove the pan from the heat.

Lay the sheets of filo pastry on a clean work surface and cut each one lengthways into three long strips, and then cut each strip in half widthways, so you end up with 42 squares.

Lightly brush a pastry square with melted butter and place a piece of Brie, a teaspoon of cranberry sauce and some pine nuts near one end, leaving some space on either side. Fold the edge of the pastry over the filling and roll up like a cigar into a cylinder. Gently twist the pastry at each end to make a 'cracker'. Place on the lined baking tray and repeat with the remaining pastry, Brie, cranberry sauce and pine nuts.

Brush the crackers with the rest of the melted butter and sprinkle with sesame seeds. Bake in the preheated oven for 10 minutes, or until crisp and golden brown.

Serve warm with chives tied round the pinched ends of the crackers, if wished.

VARIATIONS
- Instead of pine nuts, use chopped walnuts.
- Substitute Camembert or goat's cheese for the Brie.

CRISPY VEGAN 'SAUSAGE' ROLLS

///

This is a delicious vegan twist on traditional sausage rolls. Use a brand of puff pastry that is suitable for vegans – check the label before buying to make sure it does not contain butter or animal fats. And the same goes for the pesto; many manufacturers now produce vegan alternatives.

MAKES 16
PREP 20 MINUTES
COOK 35–40 MINUTES

2 tbsp olive oil
1 onion, finely chopped
3 garlic cloves, crushed
1 small red chilli, deseeded and diced
8 sage leaves, finely chopped
2 x 200g (14oz) tins white beans, e.g. cannellini or butterbeans (lima beans), rinsed and drained
½ tsp freshly grated nutmeg
grated zest and juice of ½ lemon
375g (13oz) pack of vegan ready-rolled puff pastry
2 tbsp vegan green pesto
almond milk, for brushing
sea salt and freshly ground black pepper
vegan tomato ketchup, to serve (optional)

Preheat the oven to 200°C (180°C fan)/400°F/gas 6. Line a baking tray with baking parchment.

Heat the oil in a saucepan set over a low heat and cook the onion, garlic and chilli, stirring occasionally, for 10 minutes, until softened. Add the sage and cook for 1 minute, then stir in the beans, nutmeg and lemon zest. Cook gently for 5 minutes and stir in the lemon juice.

Season to taste with salt and pepper, then mash coarsely with a potato masher. Don't overdo it – the filling should have some texture to it.

Cut the puff pastry sheet in half lengthways into 2 rectangles. Lightly brush each one with the pesto, leaving a border around the edge.

Divide the white bean mixture into 2 equal-sized portions and shape each one into a long cylinder. Place, slightly in from the edge, on the long side of each pastry rectangle. Dampen the other long edge with almond milk. Fold the long edge nearest the filling over it and then roll up to completely enclose it, ending up with the join underneath.

Slice each long roll into 8 pieces. Brush each one with almond milk and prick the top with a fork. Place on the baking tray.

Bake for 20–25 minutes, or until puffed up, crisp and golden brown. Serve hot or cold with ketchup (if wished).

BAKED TRUFFLE AND PARMESAN FRIES

//

These fries may not be very festive, but they are seriously good and worthy of a special occasion. They go down a storm at parties or served with pre-dinner drinks. We've baked ours in the oven to make them healthier. For the best results, you need to use floury potatoes, such as King Edwards, Maris Piper or Idaho russets.

SERVES 10–12
PREP 15 MINUTES
SOAK 20 MINUTES
COOK 30 MINUTES

8 large floury potatoes (see above)
3 tbsp olive oil
1 tsp dried thyme, oregano or rosemary
1 tsp sea salt
truffle oil, for drizzling
4 tbsp grated vegetarian Parmesan-style cheese, plus extra to serve

Peel the potatoes and cut them into even-sized 4mm (¼ inch) thick sticks. Place them in a bowl of ice-cold water and set aside for 20 minutes.

Meanwhile, preheat the oven to 220°C (200°C fan)/425°F/gas 7. Line 2 large baking trays with baking parchment.

Remove the potatoes from the soaking water and pat dry with kitchen paper (paper towels). Toss them in the olive oil and spread them out, not too close together, on the lined baking trays.

Bake in the preheated oven for 30 minutes, turning them halfway, or until crisp and golden brown.

Sprinkle the hot fries with the dried herbs and salt and drizzle them with truffle oil. Toss them in the grated Parmesan and serve immediately, piled up on a serving plate, sprinkled with more Parmesan.

TIP: You can use black or white truffle oil.

VARIATIONS
- Sprinkle the cooked fries with some crushed garlic or garlic granules.
- Serve sprinkled with freshly chopped flat-leaf parsley.
- Use sweet potatoes to make the fries.
- After adding the cheese, pop the fries back into the oven for a few minutes until the cheese melts.
- Serve with a dip, a bowl of garlic mayo or even ketchup.

FESTIVE LIGHT MEALS

BUTTERNUT SQUASH CHOWDER

//

This creamy soup is very filling and makes a good meal-in-a-bowl lunch or supper on a chilly midwinter day. Vegans can use dairy-free oat or nut milk to make the soup.

SERVES 4
PREP 20 MINUTES
COOK 35–40 MINUTES

1 tbsp olive oil
1 onion, finely chopped
1 celery stick, diced
4 large garlic cloves, crushed
2 leeks, trimmed and thinly sliced
900g (2lb) butternut squash, peeled, deseeded and cut into 2.5cm (1 inch) cubes
1 large potato, peeled and cubed
1 heaped tbsp plain (all-purpose) flour
600ml (1 pint/2½ cups) milk
150ml (¼ pint/generous ½ cup) vegetable stock
1 bay leaf
a good pinch of freshly grated nutmeg
250g (9oz) tin sweetcorn in water, drained
200g (7oz) spinach leaves, washed and roughly shredded
a handful of flat-leaf parsley, finely chopped
sea salt and freshly ground black pepper

Heat the oil in a large saucepan set over a low to medium heat and cook the onion, celery, garlic and leeks, stirring occasionally, for 5 minutes. Add the squash and potato and cook for 5 minutes.

Stir in the flour, then cook for 2 minutes without browning. Add the milk and stock, a little at a time, together with the bay leaf and nutmeg, and stir until smooth.

Bring to the boil, stirring constantly, and then reduce the heat to low. Add the sweetcorn and simmer gently for 15–20 minutes, or until the vegetables are cooked and tender.

Blitz half of the soup to a purée in a food processor or blender. Return to the pan and stir into the chunky soup. Add the spinach and heat gently for 4–5 minutes until it wilts into the soup and turns bright green. Stir in the parsley and season to taste with salt and pepper.

Ladle the hot soup into shallow bowls and serve immediately with some crusty bread.

TIP: This soup freezes well for up to 3 months.

VARIATIONS
· Add some roasted carrots or baby plum tomatoes.
· Use pumpkin instead of squash.
· Add a diced red chilli.
· Serve with a bowl of grated cheese for people to help themselves.
· Stir in some crème fraîche just before serving.

SPICED WINTER ROOTS SOUP

//

This warmly spiced soup is made with a selection of seasonal root vegetables and served drizzled with hot chilli oil. It freezes well, so you can make it ahead of time and reheat it for family and friends over the Christmas holiday.

SERVES 6
PREP 20 MINUTES
COOK 30 MINUTES

2 tbsp olive oil
1 large onion, finely chopped
2 celery sticks, diced
2.5cm (1 inch) piece of fresh root
   ginger, peeled and diced
400g (14oz) carrots, thinly sliced
400g (14oz) parsnips, thinly
   sliced
400g (14oz) swede (rutabaga),
   cubed
2 garlic cloves, crushed
1.2 litres (2 pints/5 cups)
   vegetable stock
1 bay leaf
a good pinch of dried oregano
1 tsp ground cumin
1 tsp ground turmeric
½ tsp ground cinnamon
½ tsp ground nutmeg
100ml (3½oz/scant ½ cup) plant-
   based milk, e.g. oat milk
sea salt and freshly ground black
   pepper

CHILLI OIL DRIZZLE
½ tsp crushed dried chilli flakes
2–3 tbsp olive oil

Heat the oil in a large saucepan set over a low to medium heat. Cook the onion, celery, ginger, carrots, parsnips and swede, stirring occasionally, for 10 minutes, or until softened. Add the garlic and cook for 1 minute.

Add the vegetable stock, bay leaf and oregano and bring to the boil. Reduce the heat and simmer gently for 15 minutes, or until the vegetables are cooked and tender. Remove the bay leaf.

Blitz the soup in batches in a blender or food processor until thick and smooth.

Return the soup to the pan and stir in the ground spices and the milk. Reheat gently over a low heat, stirring occasionally. If the soup is too thick for your liking, just thin it with some more milk until you get the right consistency. Season to taste.

Make the chilli oil: mix the chilli flakes and olive oil. Ladle the hot soup into 6 serving bowls and drizzle with the chilli oil.

VARIATIONS
- Add some celeriac, sweet potato or squash.
- Serve sprinkled with chopped parsley or coriander (cilantro).

PUMPKIN AND BUTTERBEAN SOUP

//

This healthy soup is very filling and warming on a cold day. We've topped ours with crushed tortilla chips and grated vegan cheese but anything goes, so why not sprinkle with crispy fried croûtons or swirl in a spoonful of dairy-free yoghurt with a dash of harissa or hot sauce.

SERVES 6
PREP 15 MINUTES
COOK 35–40 MINUTES

2 tbsp olive oil
1 large onion, finely chopped
3 garlic cloves, crushed
2 carrots, thinly sliced
1kg (2¼lb) pumpkin, peeled, deseeded and cubed
1 red chilli, deseeded and diced
1 tsp smoked paprika
1 tsp ground turmeric
½ tsp ground nutmeg
1.2 litres (2 pints/5 cups) hot vegetable stock
1 large potato, diced
400g (14oz) tin butterbeans (lima beans), rinsed and drained
sea salt and freshly ground black pepper

TO SERVE
chopped flat-leaf parsley, for sprinkling
50g (2oz) tortilla chips, coarsely crushed
50g (2oz/½ cup) grated vegan cheese

Heat the oil in a large saucepan set over a low to medium heat. Cook the onion for 6–8 minutes until it softens. Add the garlic, carrot and pumpkin and cook, stirring occasionally, for 5 minutes. Add the chilli and ground spices and cook for 1 minute.

Pour in the hot stock and bring to the boil. Reduce the heat to low, add the potato and simmer gently for 15–20 minutes, or until the vegetables are cooked and tender. Add half of the beans to the soup.

Blitz the soup in batches, in a blender or food processor, until smooth. Alternatively, purée the soup in the pan, off the heat, with a hand-held electric blender.

Return the soup to the pan and stir in the remaining beans. Season to taste with salt and pepper and heat through gently over a low heat.

Ladle the hot soup into 6 serving bowls and serve sprinkled with parsley, the tortilla chips and grated cheese.

VARIATIONS
- Use tinned cannellini or haricot beans instead of butterbeans.
- Substitute butternut squash or sweet potato for the pumpkin.
- Vegetarians can top the soup with grated Cheddar or Swiss cheese.
- Use crushed dried chilli flakes if you don't have a fresh chilli to hand.

Tip: Only remove the filo pastry sheets one at a time, as and when you need them, and keep the unused sheets covered with a damp tea towel to stop them drying out.

SPANAKOPITA CATHERINE WHEELS

//

These dairy-free spanakopita coiled spirals are eaten in Greece in the weeks before Christmas during Advent when many people fast and abstain from foods that come from a blood animal. They look sensational, taste delicious and reheat well in the oven.

MAKES 4
PREP 30 MINUTES
COOK 1 HOUR

1kg (2¼lb) spinach leaves, washed, trimmed and hard stalks removed
4 tbsp olive oil, plus extra for brushing
3 large leeks, trimmed and chopped
1 onion, finely chopped
2 garlic cloves, crushed
a bunch of spring onions (scallions), thinly sliced
a bunch of dill, finely chopped
a handful of flat-leaf parsley, finely chopped
½ tsp freshly grated nutmeg
a good squeeze of lemon juice
12 sheets of filo (phyllo) pastry
sea salt and freshly ground black pepper

VARIATIONS
• Add kale or spring greens to the filling.
• Mix crumbled vegan cheese into the filling.
• Vegetarians can add feta and a beaten egg to the spinach filling.

Preheat the oven to 190°C (170°C fan)/375°F/gas 5.

Put the spinach leaves in a colander and pour 1–2 kettles of boiling water over the top so the spinach wilts and turns bright green. Drain well, pressing down with a saucer to squeeze out any excess moisture. Chop the spinach coarsely.

Heat the oil in a large frying pan (skillet) set over a low to medium heat and cook the leeks and onion for 10 minutes, or until tender. Add the garlic and spring onions and cook for 2 minutes. Stir in the herbs, spinach, nutmeg, lemon juice and some salt and pepper.

Unroll the filo pastry and remove the top sheet. Lightly brush it with olive oil and place another sheet on top. Brush with oil and place a third sheet on top of the second so you have a stack of 3 sheets.

Take one-quarter of the spinach filling mixture and shape it into a long, thin cylinder. Place it along one long side of the filo pastry rectangle, leaving a 2.5cm (1 inch) border along the edge. Fold the pastry over the filling and then roll up like a cigar into a stuffed long cylinder.

Place it, seam-side down, on a work surface and, starting from one end, coil it round into a spiral shape (like a snail). Brush lightly with oil as you go along, so the coils stick together. Lift it carefully onto a lightly oiled baking sheet and brush with more oil. Repeat with the remaining filo pastry sheets and filling, so you end up with 4 spirals.

Bake in the preheated oven for 40–45 minutes, or until the pastry is crisp and golden brown. Serve hot, lukewarm or at room temperature for the best flavour.

VEGAN SEITAN WRAPS

///

Plant-based wraps and gyros are becoming all the rage. These delicious chilli seitan ones are not only high in protein but also very filling. The green lettuce, red onion and tomatoes make them look very festive.

SERVES 4
PREP 15 MINUTES
MARINATE 10 MINUTES
COOK 25–30 MINUTES

500g (1lb 2oz) seitan, cut into thin strips
4 large pita breads or wraps
250g (9oz/1 cup) vegan tzatziki
a few crisp cos (romaine) lettuce leaves, shredded
4 ripe tomatoes, sliced or coarsely chopped
1 red onion, thinly sliced
chopped flat-leaf parsley, for sprinkling
smoked paprika, for dusting

MARINADE
1 garlic clove, crushed
½ tsp crushed dried chilli flakes
1 tsp dried oregano
1 tsp ground cumin
1 tsp ground coriander
½ tsp cayenne pepper
½ tsp freshly ground black pepper
¼ tsp sea salt
grated zest and juice of 1 lemon
4 tbsp olive oil
120ml (4fl oz/½ cup) water

Preheat the oven to 200°C (180°C fan)/400°F/gas 6.

Make the marinade: mix all the ingredients together in a bowl and add the seitan. Stir gently and leave to marinate for 10 minutes.

Transfer to an ovenproof dish or roasting pan and cook in the preheated oven for 25–30 minutes, or until the seitan is golden brown and crispy on top.

Warm the pita breads or wraps for 5 minutes in the oven. Smear them with tzatziki and add the seitan, lettuce, tomato and onion. Sprinkle with parsley and dust with smoked paprika, then roll up in some baking parchment or kitchen foil to help hold the filling in place. Eat immediately.

> **TIP:** You can make your own vegan tzatziki by stirring diced cucumber, crushed garlic, sea salt, chopped dill and mint into dairy-free yoghurt.

VARIATIONS
• Use crispy fried tofu or vegan halloumi instead of seitan.
• Add some roasted squash, pumpkin or sweet potato.
• Use diced fresh red chilli instead of dried chilli flakes.
• Vegetarians can crumble some feta over the seitan and salad.

FESTIVE TOFU TOASTIE

///

This toasted sandwich is healthy and delicious and makes a good light meal or a tasty snack after all the rich festive food.

SERVES 4
PREP 15 MINUTES
COOK 4–8 MINUTES

400g (14oz) extra-firm tofu, pressed (see page 67)
2 tbsp cornflour (cornstarch)
2 tbsp sunflower oil
8 slices of wholegrain or multiseed bread
1 ripe avocado, peeled, stoned (pitted) and coarsely mashed
4 tbsp vegan mayo
2 ripe tomatoes, sliced
4 heaped tsp cranberry sauce
a few crisp lettuce leaves
sea salt and freshly ground black pepper

Cut the tofu into slices and dust them lightly with cornflour. Season with salt and pepper.

Heat the oil in a frying pan (skillet) set over a medium heat and cook the tofu, in batches, for 1–2 minutes each side until crisp and golden. Remove with a slotted spoon and drain on kitchen paper (paper towels).

Lightly toast the bread and spread 4 slices with the mashed avocado. Spread the remaining slices with the vegan mayo.

Place the sliced tomatoes on top of the avocado and cover with the hot fried tofu. Drizzle with the cranberry sauce and then add the lettuce. Top with the remaining toasted bread and cut the sandwiches in half or into quarters. Serve immediately while the tofu is hot.

VARIATIONS
· Add some crunchy pomegranate seeds.
· Add some roasted red and green (bell) peppers.
· Use fried vegan halloumi instead of tofu.

SPROUTS AND SWEET POTATO MAC 'N CHEESE

///

Adding sweet potatoes and leftover sprouts to a macaroni cheese not only makes it very colourful but also transforms it into the ultimate comfort food. Instead of the usual Cheddar, we've used grated Parmesan to give it a real Italian flavour.

SERVES 4
PREP 15 MINUTES
COOK 40–45 MINUTES

450g (1lb) sweet potatoes, peeled and cubed
225g (8oz/2¼ cups) macaroni (dry weight)
350g (12oz) cooked Brussels sprouts, halved or quartered
sea salt and freshly ground black pepper

CHEESE SAUCE
75g (3oz/scant ½ cup) butter
50g (2oz/½ cup) plain (all-purpose) flour
500ml (17fl oz/generous 2 cups) milk
2 tsp English or Dijon mustard
200g (7oz/2 cups) grated vegetarian Parmesan-style cheese

TIP: If you don't have any leftover sprouts, cook some in a pan of boiling water for 4 minutes, or until just tender.

Preheat the oven to 190°C (170°C fan)/375°F/gas 5.

Cook the sweet potatoes in a pan of salted boiling water for 10 minutes, or until tender. Drain and then transfer to a bowl and crush them with a fork. Don't mash them to a purée – you want them to retain some texture.

Meanwhile, cook the macaroni according to the instructions on the packet. Drain well and transfer to a bowl or return to the warm pan. Gently stir in the sweet potatoes.

Make the cheese sauce: melt the butter in a pan set over a low heat. Add the flour and cook for 2–3 minutes, stirring, until you have a smooth paste. Gradually whisk in the milk, beating until it's all added and free of lumps. Turn up the heat and bring to the boil, stirring all the time, until thickened, smooth and glossy. Reduce the heat and cook for 2–3 minutes, then stir in the mustard and most of the Parmesan. Season to taste.

Off the heat, gently stir the macaroni mixture and the sprouts into the sauce. Transfer to a large ovenproof dish and sprinkle with the remaining Parmesan. Bake in the preheated oven for 25–30 minutes, or until bubbling and crisp and golden brown on top. Serve with a salad.

VARIATIONS
• Use grated mature Cheddar instead of Parmesan.
• Use pumpkin or butternut squash instead of sweet potato.

BUBBLE AND SQUEAK BAKED POTATOES

//

These baked potatoes are loaded with leftover vegetables as well as fresh ones to make a bubble and squeak-style topping. For a vegan version, substitute dairy-free yoghurt and grated vegan cheese.

SERVES 4
PREP 10 MINUTES
COOK 1 HOUR 10 MINUTES

2 tbsp olive oil, plus extra for the potatoes
4 large baking potatoes
4 spring onions (scallions), chopped
2 leeks, trimmed and chopped
100g (3½oz) cooked Brussels sprouts or green cabbage, shredded
125g (4oz/½ cup) thick Greek yoghurt
100g (3½oz) Stilton, crumbled
sea salt and freshly ground black pepper

Preheat the oven to 200°C (180°C fan)/400°F/gas 6.

Lightly oil the potatoes and place them on a baking tray. Sprinkle lightly with sea salt.

Bake in the preheated oven for 1 hour or until the potatoes are cooked and feel soft when you squeeze them.

Meanwhile, heat the oil in a frying pan (skillet) set over a low to medium heat and cook the spring onion and leek, stirring occasionally, for 10 minutes, or until softened. Stir in the shredded sprouts or cabbage and season lightly with salt and pepper.

Cut the cooked potatoes in half lengthways and scoop out the flesh into a bowl. Add the yoghurt, vegetables and Stilton, and mix well together.

Spoon the mixture into the potato skins and mound it up on top. Return to the oven for 10 minutes until heated through and golden brown.

VARIATIONS
· Use any blue cheese or grated Cheddar.
· Substitute cream cheese for the yoghurt.
· Use 12 small potatoes and cook and load in the same way for serving at parties.
· Cook the leeks in butter instead of oil.

CHRISTMAS CLUB SANDWICH

//

Everybody loves a club sandwich and this one never fails to please. It tastes best eaten freshly toasted but you can wrap it up and take it to work for a packed lunch. And for an added bonus, it's a good way to use up festive leftover cheese, chestnuts and stuffing.

SERVES 4
PREP 15 MINUTES
COOK 20 MINUTES

12 slices of wholemeal, multiseed
   or granary bread
softened butter, for spreading
200g (7oz) Stilton, crumbled
4 tbsp cranberry sauce
a handful of baby spinach or
   rocket (arugula) leaves
125g (4½oz) vacuum-packed or
   cooked chestnuts, coarsely
   chopped
4 slices of cold cooked sage and
   onion stuffing
mini gherkins, dill pickles and
   potato crisps (chips), to serve

**BALSAMIC CARAMELIZED
RED ONIONS**

2 tbsp olive oil
3 red onions, peeled and cut
   into wedges
1 tbsp good-quality balsamic
   vinegar
½ tsp caster (superfine) sugar
1 tbsp water
sea salt and freshly ground black
   pepper

Make the balsamic caramelized red onions: heat the oil in a frying pan (skillet) set over a medium heat. Cook the onion wedges, turning occasionally, for 12–15 minutes until tender and starting to caramelize. Add the balsamic vinegar and sugar plus the water and cook for 5 minutes, or until the onions are dark and sweet. Season with salt and pepper.

Lightly toast the bread and thinly spread with butter.

Top 4 slices with the crumbled Stilton, pressing it down gently, and then cover with the cranberry sauce and spinach or rocket.

Cover with 4 slices of toast, buttered-side down, and top with the caramelized red onions, chestnuts and stuffing, then cover with the remaining slices of toast, buttered side down.

Cut each club sandwich in half or into quarters and secure with cocktail sticks or wooden toothpicks. Serve with mini gherkins or dill pickles and potato crisps.

VARIATIONS
• If you're in a hurry, use shop-bought caramelized red onion chutney.
• Add some sliced spring onions (scallions) or tomatoes.
• Use sliced Brie or goat's cheese instead of Stilton.
• Add some roasted red, yellow and green (bell) peppers.

STILTON AND CARAMELIZED ONION TARTS

//

The caramelized onions add a hit of sweetness to these delicious savoury tarts. You can prepare and assemble them in advance and just pop them into the oven to finish them off later in the day.

SERVES 4
PREP 20 MINUTES
COOK 40–50 MINUTES

400g (14oz) shortcrust pastry (pie crust)
2 tbsp olive oil
2 red onions, thinly sliced
400g (14oz) swede (rutabaga), cubed
a few sprigs of parsley, chopped
2 medium free-range eggs, beaten
50g (2oz) Stilton, crumbled
sea salt and freshly ground black pepper
cranberry or redcurrant sauce, to serve

Preheat the oven to 190°C (170°C fan)/375°F/gas 5.

Roll out the pastry and use to line 4 x 12cm (5 inch) tartlet tins (pans). Prick the bases and fill with crumpled baking parchment or kitchen foil and baking beans. Place on a baking tray and bake in the preheated oven for 15–20 minutes until firm and golden. Remove the paper or foil and beans.

Meanwhile, heat the oil in a saucepan set over a low to medium heat and cook the onion, stirring occasionally, for 20–25 minutes until tender, golden and starting to caramelize.

While the onion is cooking, boil the swede in a pan of water for 12–15 minutes, or until tender. Drain well and then coarsely crush with a fork.

Mix together the onion, swede and parsley. Season to taste and set aside to cool before stirring in the beaten egg.

Divide the mixture into the pastry cases and crumble the Stilton over the top. Bake in the preheated oven for 20–25 minutes until set and golden brown.

Serve the tarts with some salad and cranberry or redcurrant sauce on the side.

VARIATIONS
- Use puff pastry instead of shortcrust.
- Substitute butternut squash or pumpkin for the swede.
- Use mini cocktail tartlet cases (shells) instead and serve as canapés.
- Use goat's cheese or grated Cheddar instead of the Stilton.

MERRY
MAINS

ROASTED RED ONION AND MUSHROOM TOAD

//

You can make a crisp vegan Yorkshire pudding with water or non-dairy milk plus aquafaba (see below) to replace the eggs in a traditional batter. This 'toad-in-the-hole' is very versatile, and you can adapt it easily to make use of other vegetables.

SERVES 4
PREP 20 MINUTES
COOK 40–45 MINUTES

2 leeks, trimmed and thinly sliced
1 large red onion, thinly sliced
4 Portobello mushrooms
4 tbsp olive oil
4 sprigs of cherry tomatoes on the vine
sea salt and freshly ground black pepper
vegan green pesto, for drizzling

BATTER
175g (6oz/1¾ cups) self-raising (self-rising) flour
1 tsp baking powder
½ tsp sea salt
¼ tsp ground turmeric
¼ tsp Dijon mustard
4 tbsp aquafaba (see note)
300ml (½ pint/1¼ cups) water or plant-based milk
a small handful of parsley, chopped

NOTE: Aquafaba is the liquid from a tin of chickpeas (garbanzos). Vegetarians can make a traditional batter with milk and eggs.

Preheat the oven to 220°C (200°C fan)/425°F/gas mark 7.

Make the batter: sift the flour and baking powder into a bowl and stir in the salt and turmeric. Make a well in the centre.

In a separate bowl, whisk together the mustard, aquafaba and water or milk. Pour into the well and whisk until you have a smooth batter that is bubbly but free from lumps. Stir in the parsley, then pour the batter into a jug and set aside for 15 minutes.

Meanwhile, put the leeks, red onion and mushrooms, open-side down, in a large roasting pan. Season with salt and pepper and drizzle with the oil. Cook in the preheated oven for 10 minutes. Turn the mushrooms over and cook for 5 minutes more.

Quickly pour the batter over the vegetables and place the tomatoes on top. Return to the oven immediately and cook for 25–30 minutes or until the batter is well risen, crisp on top and golden brown. Do not open the oven door while the toad is cooking, or it may collapse.

Serve immediately, cut into wedges and drizzled with pesto, with a crisp salad or some green vegetables.

VARIATIONS
- Add some shelled peas or shredded spinach.
- Use chestnut mushrooms and cubes of roasted pumpkin or squash.
- Add some vegan 'sausages'.
- Serve with vegan gravy.

ROASTED CAULIFLOWER 'STEAKS' AND TOMATO SAUCE

//

Roasted cauliflower 'steaks' are appetizingly golden brown and surprisingly filling. We've served them in a pool of tomato sauce with green beans for a festive meal. For a more traditional approach, omit the tomato sauce and serve with vegan stuffing balls, Brussels sprouts and cranberry sauce.

SERVES 4
PREP 15 MINUTES
COOK 35–40 MINUTES

1 large cauliflower, stalk trimmed and leaves discarded
1 tbsp olive oil, plus extra for brushing
1 tsp crushed dried chilli flakes
4 tbsp toasted flaked almonds
sea salt and freshly ground black pepper
fine green beans and crispy roast potatoes, to serve

TOMATO SAUCE
3 tbsp olive oil
1 large onion, diced
3 garlic cloves, crushed
450g (1lb) ripe sweet tomatoes, chopped
a pinch of sugar
a splash of balsamic vinegar

Preheat the oven to 200°C (180°C fan)/400°F/gas 6. Line a large baking tray with kitchen foil or baking parchment.

Slice the cauliflower through the stem into 4 x 2.5cm (1 inch) thick 'steaks'. Heat the olive oil in a large frying pan (skillet) set over a high heat. Add the cauliflower steaks, one at a time, to the hot pan and cook for 4 minutes, turning them halfway through, or until they start to colour.

Place the cauliflower steaks on the lined baking tray and brush lightly with more olive oil. Sprinkle with chilli flakes, sea salt and black pepper. Roast in the preheated oven for 20 minutes, or until tender, golden brown and slightly charred round the edges.

Meanwhile, make the tomato sauce: pour the oil into the pan and reduce the heat to low to medium. Cook the onion, stirring occasionally, for 6–8 minutes, or until softened. Add the garlic and cook for 1 minute, then stir in the tomatoes and sugar and cook for 5 minutes, or until the mixture reduces and thickens. Add a splash of balsamic vinegar, plus salt and pepper to taste. Transfer the mixture to a blender or food processor and blitz until smooth.

Divide the tomato sauce among 4 serving plates, spreading it out in a circle on each plate. Place a roasted cauliflower steak in the centre of each circle. Scatter with the toasted almonds and serve immediately with green beans and roast potatoes.

VARIATIONS
- Drizzle the cauliflower with some pesto.
- Sprinkle with chopped fresh herbs.
- If you don't have fresh tomatoes for the sauce, use tinned plum ones.

SPINACH AND CHESTNUT ROULADE

///

This healthy roulade is light and delicious – perfect for when you want a change from rich foods and heavy meals. It doesn't take long to make and looks impressive, making it a good choice for Boxing Day lunch or even for Christmas Day.

SERVES 4–6
PREP 30 MINUTES
COOK 15 MINUTES

400g (14oz) spinach leaves,
    washed and trimmed
a pinch of freshly grated nutmeg
2 tbsp grated vegetarian
    Parmesan-style cheese
4 medium free-range eggs,
    separated
250g (9oz/generous 1 cup) soft
    cream cheese
100g (3½oz/¾ cup) vacuum-
    packed or cooked chestnuts,
    finely chopped
a bunch of chives, snipped
grated zest of 1 lemon
sea salt and freshly ground black
    pepper

MUSHROOM SAUCE
2 tbsp olive oil
1 small onion, chopped
2 garlic cloves, crushed
400g (14oz) mushrooms, sliced
240ml (8fl oz/1 cup) crème
    fraîche
a handful of parsley, chopped

Preheat the oven to 190°C (170°C fan)/375°F/gas 5. Line a 30 x 25cm (12 x 10 inch) Swiss roll tin with non-stick baking parchment.

Put the damp spinach in a saucepan and cook, covered, over a low heat for 2–3 minutes, shaking the pan once or twice, until the leaves wilt and turn bright green. Drain in a colander and press out any excess moisture with a saucer.

Chop the spinach finely, then transfer to a bowl and mix in the nutmeg, Parmesan, egg yolks and some seasoning.

Whisk the egg whites in a clean, dry bowl until they stand in stiff peaks. Fold them gently with a metal spoon into the spinach mixture, using a figure-of-eight motion. Pour into the prepared tin and bake in the oven for 15 minutes, or until firm to the touch.

Meanwhile, make the mushroom sauce: heat the oil in a frying pan (skillet) over a medium heat and cook the onion, garlic and mushrooms, stirring occasionally, for 8–10 minutes until tender and golden. Stir in the crème fraîche and parsley and cook for 2–3 minutes to heat through. Season to taste.

Turn out the roulade onto a sheet of greaseproof paper and remove the lining paper. Cover with non-stick baking parchment and roll up, starting from one of the short ends.

Mix the cream cheese with the chestnuts, chives and lemon zest. Unroll the roulade, remove the baking parchment and spread with the cheesy mixture. Reroll and serve, cut into slices, with the mushroom sauce.

> **VARIATION**
> • Serve with a tomato sauce or a creamy watercress sauce.

FESTIVE FILO PARCELS

//

These individual crispy 'parcels' look pretty and colourful for a special Christmas meal. It takes a little while to assemble and fill them, but the results make it more than worth the effort.

SERVES 6
PREP 30 MINUTES
COOK 35–40 MINUTES

270g (9½oz) pack of filo (phyllo) pastry sheets (6 sheets)
olive oil or melted butter, for brushing
6 long chives
cranberry sauce, to serve
Brussels sprouts or broccoli, and carrots, to serve

FILLING
4 tbsp olive oil
1 red onion, finely chopped
3 garlic cloves, crushed
3 tsp black mustard seeds
1 tsp crushed dried chilli flakes
450g (1lb) cooked beetroot (beets), cubed
400g (14oz) spinach leaves, washed and trimmed
2 x 400g (14oz) tins chickpeas (garbanzos), rinsed and drained
3 tbsp chopped parsley
100g (3½oz) feta cheese, crumbled
sea salt and freshly ground black pepper

Preheat the oven to 200°C (180°C fan)/400°F/gas 6. Line a baking tray with baking parchment.

Make the filling: heat the oil in a frying pan (skillet) set over a low to medium heat. Cook the red onion and garlic, stirring occasionally, for 8–10 minutes, until softened. Stir in the mustard seeds and chilli flakes and cook for 2 minutes. Season to taste with salt and pepper.

Blitz the beetroot in a food processor until thick and smooth.

Put the spinach in a colander and pour 1–2 kettles of boiling water over it until it wilts and turns bright green. Let the water drain away and press out any excess moisture with a saucer. Chop the spinach coarsely.

In a bowl, gently mix the spicy onion mixture with the spinach, chickpeas and the puréed beetroot. Do not over-mix – you want the colours to stay separate but to blend a little. Lastly, fold in the parsley and feta.

Cut a filo pastry sheet in half and then in half again, so you have 4 square pieces. Brush one square with oil or melted butter and cover with another square. Layer up the other 2 pieces on top, brushing with oil or butter in between them. Put one-sixth of the filling mixture in the centre and pull up the edges of the pastry around it to make a 'money purse' shape, twisting the top and pinching the edges together to seal in the filling. Repeat in the same way with the remaining filo sheets and filling.

Place the parcels on the lined baking sheet and brush them lightly with oil or butter. Bake for 20–25 minutes until crisp and golden brown. Remove from the oven and tie a single chive in a bow around the neck of each parcel. Serve the parcels with cranberry sauce, green vegetables and carrots.

BUTTERNUT SQUASH AND CRANBERRY CHEESY PLAIT

///

A crisp, golden puff pastry plaited (braided) pie always makes an impressive centrepiece and this one is no exception. Vegans can use vegan puff pastry and cheese and glaze the pie with aquafaba (see page 28) or milk before baking.

SERVES 6
PREP 25 MINUTES
COOK 55 MINUTES

600g (1lb 5oz) butternut squash, peeled, deseeded and cubed
2 tbsp olive oil, plus extra for drizzling
2 red onions, thinly sliced
2 garlic cloves, crushed
1 tsp thyme leaves
200g (7oz) spinach leaves, washed and coarsely chopped
200g (7oz) bottled roasted red (bell) peppers in oil, drained and cut into pieces
2 tbsp cranberry sauce
200g (7oz/2 cups) grated Cheddar cheese
375g (13oz) pack of ready-rolled puff pastry
1 medium free-range egg, beaten
sea salt and freshly ground black pepper
sesame seeds and nigella (kalonji) seeds, for sprinkling

VARIATION
• Use crumbled feta or blue cheese.

Preheat the oven to 200°C (180°C fan)/400°F/gas 6.

Place the squash on a baking tray (sheet) and drizzle with olive oil. Season lightly with salt and pepper and roast in the preheated oven for 25 minutes, or until tender but not mushy.

Meanwhile, make the filling: heat the oil in a frying pan (skillet) set over a low heat and cook the onion, garlic and thyme, stirring, for 15–20 minutes until tender and lightly caramelized.

Stir in the spinach and cook for 2 minutes, or until it wilts. Remove from the heat and add the roasted red peppers and cranberry sauce. Season lightly with salt and pepper, then gently mix in the roasted butternut squash and grated cheese.

Roll out the pastry on a lightly floured surface to a larger rectangle if needed – it should be about 3mm (⅛ inch) thick and fit a baking tray (sheet) lined with baking parchment. Spoon the filling lengthways down the centre of the pastry.

Cut the pastry diagonally at 2cm (¾ inch) intervals all the way down on both sides from the filling to the edge to create strips. Fold the strips up and over the filling, alternating from side to side, like a plait (braid). Lightly brush the pastry with beaten egg and sprinkle with sesame and nigella seeds.

Bake in the preheated oven for 30 minutes or until the pastry is puffed up, golden brown and crisp. Serve cut into slices.

TIP: Homemade cranberry sauce works best as the cranberries keep their shape better. Add the sauce to the pie or, if preferred, serve it as an accompaniment.

MUSHROOM AND BEETROOT WELLINGTON

//

This makes an impressive centrepiece for your special festive lunch or dinner. If you can find a really large cylindrical-shaped beetroot (beet), it will be easier to assemble the Wellington and will look nice and neat when you slice it. However, you can use two medium-sized beetroots or four small ones instead and place them in a line, end to end, within the spinach wrapping on top of the duxelles and pastry.

SERVES 6
PREP 40 MINUTES
COOK 1 HOUR

1 large (about 500g/1lb 2oz) raw
   cylindrical beetroot (beets),
   washed and trimmed
175g (6oz) large spinach leaves,
   washed and trimmed
375g (13oz) pack of ready-rolled
   vegan puff pastry
2 tbsp aquafaba (see page 28)
2 tbsp plant-based milk
poppy seeds, for sprinkling
mustard, horseradish or cranberry
   sauce, to serve

Put the beetroot in a pan of simmering water and cook for 25–30 minutes, or until the beetroot is cooked and tender. Drain and set aside until it is cool enough to handle, then peel off the skin.

Meanwhile, make the mushroom duxelles: heat the olive oil in a frying pan (skillet) set over a medium heat and cook the shallots, stirring occasionally, for 5 minutes, or until softened. Add the garlic and mushrooms and cook for 5 minutes, or until tender and the moisture from the mushrooms evaporates. Stir in the thyme and chestnuts, and season with salt and pepper to taste.

Transfer to a blender or food processor and pulse until you have a slightly chunky paste.

Preheat the oven to 220°C (200°C fan)/425°F/gas 7. Line a baking tray with baking parchment.

Bring a pan of water to the boil and drop in the spinach leaves. Blanch for 30 seconds, then remove with a slotted spoon. Drain and then place in a bowl of iced water for 1 minute. Drain well and pat dry with kitchen paper (paper towels).

Unroll the pastry and lay it flat on a large board. Spread the mushroom duxelles paste over it, leaving a 2.5cm (1 inch) border around the edge.

Wrap the peeled beetroot in the spinach leaves and place in the centre of the pastry on top of the mushroom duxelles paste. The length of the beetroot should line up with the long sides of the rectangle. If you are using more than one beetroot, overlap the spinach leaves in a row and then put the beetroots end to end on top and cover them with the leaves.

MUSHROOM DUXELLES

1 tbsp olive oil

4 shallots, diced

3 garlic cloves, crushed

500g (1lb 2oz) chestnut
　mushrooms, trimmed and
　diced

leaves stripped from 4 sprigs of
　thyme

200g (7oz/1½ cups) vacuum-
　packed or cooked chestnuts,
　chopped

sea salt and freshly ground black
　pepper

Mix the aquafaba with the milk and use some of it to lightly brush the pastry border all the way round. Fold one long side of the pastry over the top of the beetroot and roll up to enclose the filling. Press along the join to seal it. Turn the pastry parcel over, seam-side down, and seal the ends of the pastry and tuck them underneath.

Place on the lined baking tray and brush with the remaining aquafaba mixture. Score the top 2–3 times with a sharp knife. If you have any pastry trimmings leftover, cut out some decorative stars and place them on top. Sprinkle lightly with poppy seeds.

Bake in the preheated oven for 30 minutes, or until the pastry is puffy, crisp and appetizingly golden brown. Serve immediately, cut into slices and serve with mustard, horseradish sauce or cranberry sauce.

VARIATIONS

- Use walnuts instead of chestnuts in the duxelles.
- Add some green pesto before wrapping the beetroot in the spinach.
- Vegetarians can add some softened blue cheese to the mushroom mixture.

BUTTERNUT SQUASH FESTIVE WREATHS

//

These colourful puff pastry wreaths are easier to assemble than they look and make a fabulous centrepiece for Christmas Day lunch or dinner. You could even roll out the puff pastry trimmings to make 'stars' and use them to decorate the top of the wreaths (see Note).

SERVES 4–6
PREP 30 MINUTES
COOK 50–60 MINUTES

900g (2lb) butternut squash, peeled, deseeded and cut into small cubes
2 red onions, thinly sliced
2 tbsp olive oil
2 tbsp maple syrup
4 unpeeled whole garlic cloves
2 x 375g (13oz) packs of ready-rolled puff pastry
100g (3½oz) baby spinach leaves
85g (3oz/scant ½ cup) shelled pistachios
1 red chilli, deseeded and diced
100g (3½oz/1 cup) grated Cheddar cheese
4 tsp green pesto
4 tsp cranberry sauce
1 medium free-range egg, beaten
sea salt and freshly ground black pepper

NOTE: To make decorative pastry stars, roll out the pastry trimmings and stamp out some stars with a star-shaped pastry cutter. Attach to the pastry wreath with beaten egg before baking.

Preheat the oven to 200°C (180°C fan)/400°F/gas 6. Line 2 baking trays with baking parchment.

Place the squash and red onions on 2 other baking trays and drizzle with the olive oil and maple syrup. Tuck the garlic cloves in between, season lightly with salt and pepper and roast in the preheated oven for 30–40 minutes, or until tender and starting to caramelize.

Meanwhile, roll out the pastry sheets, if needed, until they are about 6mm (¼ inch) thick and big enough to cut a large round from. Place each one on a lined baking tray. Using a 27cm (11 inch) flan tin or dinner plate as a guide, place it on top of each puff pastry sheet and cut round it to make a large circle. Set aside the pastry trimmings. Next, use a smaller plate to lightly score out an inner circle in the centre of each round. Use a sharp knife to cut through the pastry of the inner circle, first lengthways, then widthways, and again through the quarters to create 8 sections.

Squeeze the garlic out of the skins and stir into the hot roasted squash and onion mixture. Add the spinach and leave it to wilt slightly and soften. Place spoonfuls of the mixture in a ring around each pastry disc, avoiding the outer edge and the central star. Sprinkle with the pistachios, chilli and grated cheese. Drizzle alternately with pesto and cranberry sauce around the ring on top.

Work your way round each disc, raising the outer edge a little and pulling the point of each cut inner section over the filling towards the pastry edge. Pinch them together with your fingers to seal.

Lightly brush the pastry with beaten egg and, if using, attach some pastry stars (see opposite). Bake in the preheated oven for 20 minutes, or until puffed up, crisp and golden brown.

SWEET POTATO AND CHESTNUT FILO PARCELS

//

These pretty little filo parcels are great for parties or served as a first course on Christmas Day.
You could use grated butternut squash instead of sweet potato.

MAKES 14
PREP 25 MINUTES
COOK 15 MINUTES

1 large sweet potato, grated
400g (14oz) tin cannellini beans,
    rinsed, drained and coarsely
    crushed
100g (3½oz/¾ cup) vacuum-
    packed or cooked chestnuts,
    chopped
100g (3½oz/⅓ cup) cranberry
    sauce
a few sprigs of parsley, chopped
7 sheets of vegan filo (phyllo)
    pastry
olive or rapeseed oil, for brushing
sea salt and freshly ground black
    pepper

Preheat the oven to 200°C (180°C fan)/400°F/gas 6. Line 2
baking trays with baking parchment.

Put the sweet potato, beans, chestnuts, cranberry sauce and
parsley in a bowl. Season lightly with salt and pepper and mix
everything together.

Cut each sheet of filo pastry into 4 squares. Lightly brush one
square with oil and place another square on top at a 45-degree
angle to form a star shape. Repeat with the other sheets until you
have 14 star shapes. Brush lightly with oil and divide the sweet
potato filling among them, placing it in the centre of each star.

Gently bring the sides of each star over the filling to meet at the
top in the middle and pinch them together to seal in the filling,
and to make an attractive 'money bag' shape with the tips of the
stars pointing out.

Place the parcels on the lined baking tray and brush lightly with
oil. Bake in the preheated oven for 15 minutes or until crisp and
golden brown.

VARIATIONS
• Add some ground cinnamon or crushed dried chilli flakes
  to the filling.
• Substitute thyme or sage for the parsley.
• Stir in a little vegan cream cheese.

VEGAN XMAS CROSTINI

//

Sweet and salty is a great flavour combination, and they come together in these caramelized shallot party canapés. You can prepare the topping in advance and just reheat it prior to assembling and serving the crostini.

MAKES ABOUT 30 CROSTINI
PREP 15 MINUTES
COOK 20–25 MINUTES

3 tbsp olive oil, plus more for
  brushing
600g (1lb 5oz) shallots, peeled
  and quartered
1 tsp sugar
2 x 400g (14oz) tins white beans,
  e.g. cannellini or haricot, rinsed
  and drained
100g (3½oz/¾ cup) vacuum-
  packed or cooked chestnuts,
  chopped
a large handful of flat-leaf parsley
1 baguette (French stick), thinly
  sliced
2 garlic cloves, halved
120ml (4fl oz/½ cup) vegan green
  pesto
2 red chillies, deseeded and
  shredded
sea salt and freshly ground black
  pepper

Preheat the oven to 200°C (180°C fan)/400°F/gas 6.

Heat the olive oil in a frying pan (skillet) set over a low to medium heat. Cook the shallots, turning occasionally, for 10–15 minutes, or until softened and golden brown. Sprinkle with the sugar and continue cooking until the shallots are a deep golden colour and starting to caramelize.

Stir in the beans, chestnuts and most of the parsley. Season to taste with salt and pepper. Coarsely mash with a fork, leaving some beans whole.

Place the baguette slices on 2 baking trays and brush them lightly with olive oil. Bake in the preheated oven for about 8–10 minutes, turning them halfway through, until crisp and golden brown. Remove from the oven and rub the cut garlic cloves over one side of the bread.

Spread a little pesto over each slice and then top with the shallot and bean mixture. Sprinkle with the chillies and the remaining parsley and serve warm.

VARIATIONS
- Add some diced mushrooms to the bean mixture.
- Spread the crostini with vegan cream cheese before adding the pesto and shallot mixture.
- Add a few drops of balsamic vinegar to the caramelized shallots.

VEGAN CHRISTMAS PIZZA WREATHS

//

These pizza wreaths are a bit fiddly but if you don't want to make the dough yourself, you can buy packs of ready-rolled pizza dough or pizza bases. Brussels sprouts work surprisingly well as a pizza topping, especially when they crisp up around the edges.

SERVES 4
PREP 30 MINUTES
RISE 1–2 HOURS
COOK 35 MINUTES

200g (7oz) Brussels sprouts, trimmed and halved or quartered
1 red (bell) pepper, deseeded and diced
100g (3½oz/¾ cup) vacuum-packed or cooked chestnuts, chopped
olive oil, for drizzling
200g (7oz/2 cups) shredded vegan mozzarella
vegan green pesto, for drizzling
fried sage leaves (see opposite) and rocket (arugula), to garnish (optional)

Make the pizza bases: put the flour in a large mixing bowl with the yeast and salt. Make a well in the centre and pour in most of the warm water. Mix to a soft dough, drawing in the flour from the sides with your hand. If it's too dry, add some more warm water.

Put the ball of dough on a well-floured work surface and knead by hand for 10 minutes until smooth, silky and elastic. Place in a large lightly oiled bowl and cover with cling film (plastic wrap). Leave in a warm place for 1–2 hours until it rises and doubles in size.

Meanwhile, make the tomato sauce: heat the oil in a large frying pan (skillet) set over a low to medium heat and cook the onion, stirring occasionally, for 6–8 minutes until softened. Add the garlic and chilli and cook for 2–3 minutes, then stir in the tomatoes, tomato purée and sugar. Simmer for 10 minutes or until it reduces and thickens. Add the vinegar and seasoning to taste.

Preheat the oven to 220°C (200°C fan)/425°F/gas 7. Knock the dough down with your fist and knead it lightly. Cut into 4 pieces and roll each one out thinly into a large round, about 23cm (9 inch) diameter. Use a round metal cutter, about 7cm (3 inch) diameter, to cut out a circle in the middle. Place the pizza 'wreaths' on baking trays.

TOMATO SAUCE

2 tbsp olive oil

1 large onion, finely chopped

3 garlic cloves, crushed

1 red chilli, diced

400g (14oz) tin plum tomatoes, chopped

2 tbsp tomato purée (paste)

a good pinch of sugar

a dash of balsamic vinegar

sea salt and freshly ground black pepper

PIZZA BASES

500g (1lb 2oz/5 cups) Italian 00 flour or strong white flour, plus extra for flouring

7g (¼oz) sachet of fast-action yeast

1 tsp sea salt

300ml (½ pint/1¼ cups) warm water

Spread the tomato sauce over the pizza bases almost up to the outer edge. Scatter the sprouts, red pepper and chestnuts over the sauce and drizzle with olive oil. Sprinkle with the mozzarella and bake in the preheated oven for 15 minutes, or until the bases are cooked and crisp and the cheese has melted.

Drizzle the pizza wreaths with pesto and serve immediately, garnished with fried sage leaves and rocket (if using).

NOTE: To make fried sage leaves, just heat some extra-virgin olive oil in a frying pan (skillet) set over a medium to high heat. Add some large fresh sage leaves, a few at a time, and cook for 30 seconds or until crisp. Remove and drain on kitchen paper (paper towels), then sprinkle with a little salt.

VARIATIONS
- Use crushed dried chilli flakes instead of fresh chilli.
- Use bottled or roasted red (bell) peppers.
- Use leftover vegetables and cheese.

PARSNIP TARTE TATIN

//

This caramelized parsnip and shallot tart is much easier to make than it looks. Using a packet of ready-rolled vegan puff pastry takes all the hard work out of it. You will need a non-stick frying pan (skillet) with an ovenproof handle to make this dish. Serve with a crisp chicory or radicchio winter salad in a mustardy dressing.

SERVES 4
PREP 20 MINUTES
COOK 45–50 MINUTES

2 tbsp olive oil
450g (1lb) small to medium parsnips, peeled and cut into long wedges
200g (7oz) whole shallots, peeled
2 tbsp soft light brown sugar
2 tbsp good-quality balsamic vinegar
2 tablespoons cold water
100g (3½oz/¾ cup) vacuum-packed or cooked chestnuts, chopped
375g (13oz) pack of ready-rolled vegan puff pastry
sea salt and freshly ground black pepper

Preheat the oven to 200°C (180°C fan)/400°F/gas 6.

Heat the oil in a 23cm (9 inch) non-stick ovenproof frying pan (skillet) set over a medium heat. Add the parsnips and shallots and cook for 8–10 minutes, turning occasionally, until they are tender and golden brown. Remove the parsnips and set aside.

Add the sugar and vinegar to the shallots, along with the water, and cook over a low heat for 10 minutes, or until they start to caramelize. Remove from the heat and return the parsnips to the pan, arranging them in an attractive pattern if liked. Season lightly with salt and pepper and scatter the chestnuts over the top.

Roll out the pastry if needed to be able to cut out a circle that's a little larger than the pan. Lay it loosely over the top of the pan and tuck in the edges.

Bake in the preheated oven for 25–30 minutes, or until the pastry is puffed up and golden brown and the caramel juices are bubbling at the edges.

Remove from the oven and let the tart cool a little for 5 minutes, then, using an oven cloth to prevent you from getting burnt, place a plate upside down on top of the tart and carefully invert the pan to turn out the tart onto the plate. Serve hot.

VARIATIONS
• Use squash or sweet potatoes instead of parsnips.
• Spice it up with garam masala and some black mustard or nigella (kalonji) seeds.
• Add some thyme leaves or a diced red chilli.

CHRISTMAS SAVOURY BAKLAVA

//

You are probably familiar with the sticky, sweet squares of baklava, soaked in honey or syrup, that are served as a dessert, but did you know that you can also make a delicious savoury version? This makes a wonderful main course for Christmas Day or you can eat it at room temperature on Boxing Day.

SERVES 6
PREP 30 MINUTES
COOK 1–1¼ HOURS

900g (2lb) pumpkin or butternut squash, peeled, deseeded and diced
4 tbsp olive oil, plus extra for brushing
2 large onions, chopped
3 garlic cloves, crushed
2 red chillies, deseeded and diced
1 tsp paprika
2 tsp cumin seeds
400g (14oz) tin white beans, e.g. cannellini, rinsed and drained
2 tbsp tomato purée (paste)
1 tsp harissa paste (optional)
200g (7oz/1½cups) vacuum-packed or cooked chestnuts, chopped
200g (7oz/1¼ cups) ready-to-eat apricots, chopped
a handful of parsley, finely chopped
a handful of mint, finely chopped
9 sheets of filo (phyllo) pastry (2 x 270g/9½oz packs)

Preheat the oven to 200°C (180°C fan)/400°F/gas 6. Lightly brush a 30 x 20cm (12 x 8 inch) deep baking tin (pan) with oil.

Arrange the pumpkin or squash on a large baking tray and drizzle with 2 tablespoons of the olive oil. Season with salt and pepper and roast in the preheated oven for 20–30 minutes, until tender but not mushy.

Meanwhile, heat the remaining olive oil in a large pan set over a low to medium heat. Cook the onion and garlic, stirring occasionally, for 8–10 minutes, or until softened. Stir in the chilli, paprika and cumin seeds and cook for 1 minute.

Add the beans, tomato purée and harissa (if using) and warm through for a few minutes, crushing a few of the beans with a fork, and then stir in the chestnuts, apricots and herbs. Stir in the roasted pumpkin or squash and check the seasoning.

Reduce the oven temperature to 180°C (160°C fan)/350°F/gas 4.

Unfold the filo pastry and cover with a damp cloth to prevent it drying out. Use a sheet to cover the bottom of the baking tin. Lightly brush with melted butter and then add 2 more sheets, brushing with butter each time.

Spoon half of the bean mixture over the top in a single layer and sprinkle with half of the grated cheese. Cover with 3 more filo sheets, buttering and layering them in the same way, and spoon the rest of the bean mixture and cheese over the top.

115g (4oz/½ cup) butter, melted
200g (7oz/2 cups) grated
   vegetarian cheese, e.g.
   Graviera, Gruyère,
   Parmesan-style, Cheddar
black or white sesame seeds, for
   sprinkling
Greek thyme honey, for drizzling
sea salt and freshly ground black
   pepper
green vegetables and braised red
   cabbage, to serve

Cover with the remaining 3 filo sheets, brushing them with butter as before. Use a sharp knife to lightly score the top in a diamond pattern and brush with any remaining butter. Sprinkle with sesame seeds.

Bake in the preheated oven for 45 minutes, or until the pastry is uniformly crisp and golden brown. Remove from the oven and set aside to cool for 5 minutes.

Drizzle the honey over the baklava and serve cut into squares with green vegetables and braised red cabbage.

VARIATIONS
- Use kidney beans or chickpeas (garbanzos) instead of white beans.
- Substitute crumbled feta for the grated cheese.
- Add some chopped spinach leaves and tomatoes to the bean mixture.
- Use coriander (cilantro) instead of parsley.
- Add some crunchy chopped pistachios or walnuts.

TIP: If the filo sheets are too large for the dish, just trim them to fit.

SEASONAL SALADS AND SIDES

WINTER SHREDDED SPROUTS AND STILTON SALAD

///

This crunchy green and red salad will brighten up even the darkest winter day. The lemon juice in the dressing adds zingy, citrusy freshness and the pomegranate seeds resemble rubies. It's a great way to serve crunchy Brussels sprouts and to use up some leftover walnuts and Stilton.

SERVES 4
PREP 15 MINUTES
CHILL 30 MINUTES

300g (10oz) Brussels sprouts, trimmed and thinly shredded
2 red apples, cored and cubed
1 ripe avocado, peeled, stoned (pitted) and diced
85g (3oz/¾ cup) chopped walnuts
a handful of flat-leaf parsley, chopped
115g (4oz) Stilton cheese, cubed
seeds of ½ pomegranate

HONEY MUSTARD VINAIGRETTE
3 tbsp extra-virgin olive oil
1 tbsp apple cider vinegar
1 tsp honey mustard
juice of ½ lemon
sea salt and freshly ground black pepper

Make the honey vinaigrette: whisk all the ingredients together until well combined.

Put the shredded sprouts in a serving bowl and toss in the dressing. Cover and place in the fridge for 30 minutes to absorb the flavour of the dressing.

Add the apples, avocado, walnuts and parsley, and toss everything gently together.

Sprinkle the Stilton over the top and stir lightly. Scatter with the pomegranate seeds and serve immediately.

> **TIP:** You can use a food processor to shred the sprouts.

VARIATIONS
- Add some chopped spring onions (scallions) or red onion.
- Use pears instead of apples.
- Substitute toasted pine nuts or hazelnuts for the walnuts.

SPROUTS WITH CHESTNUTS AND BUTTERED CRUMBS

//

This is the classic way of cooking and serving Brussels sprouts, with a sprinkle of crispy golden crumbs to give them extra flavour and crunch. Boil the sprouts hard, uncovered, to retain their lovely fresh green colour.

SERVES 4
PREP 20 MINUTES
COOK 15–20 MINUTES

250g (9oz) whole chestnuts in
    their shells
500g (1lb 2oz) Brussels sprouts
30g (1oz/2 tbsp) butter
sea salt and freshly ground black
    pepper

BUTTERED CRUMBS
30g (1oz/2 tbsp) butter
50g (2oz/1 cup) fresh white
    breadcrumbs

TIP: If you don't fancy cooking and peeling the chestnuts yourself, take the easy route and use vacuum-packed cooked and peeled ones.

Nick each chestnut with a sharp knife and add to a pan of boiling water. Boil for 10 minutes and then turn off the heat. Peel the warm chestnuts, a few at a time, keeping the rest warm in the hot water. This makes them easier to peel. Chop them into large pieces and set aside.

Cut the ends off the sprouts and throw away any torn outer leaves. Cut a small cross in the base of each sprout.

Bring a large pan of lightly salted water to the boil and tip in the sprouts. Boil for 4–5 minutes or until just tender – they should retain a little crispness and bite. Do not overcook them. Drain well.

Return the sprouts to the hot pan with the butter and chestnuts and stir gently over a low to medium heat until the butter melts and everything is coated.

Meanwhile, make the buttered crumbs: melt the butter in a frying pan (skillet) set over a medium heat. Add the breadcrumbs and fry gently, tossing, until crispy and golden. Remove from the heat immediately before they turn brown.

Transfer the sprouts to a serving dish, grind over some black pepper and serve hot, sprinkled with the buttered crumbs.

VARIATIONS
- Add some grated lemon zest and chopped parsley to the breadcrumbs.
- Sauté some flaked almonds in butter until golden, and scatter over the sprouts.

HASSELBACK SQUASH WITH PECANS AND MAPLE SYRUP

//

Prepared and cooked in this way, a butternut squash makes an impressive and delicious side dish for the main course on Christmas Day. It's a little bit time-consuming to make but well worth the effort.

SERVES 6

PREP 20 MINUTES

COOK 1 HOUR

2 medium butternut squash,
   peeled
85g (3oz/⅓ cup) unsalted butter
4 tbsp maple syrup
2 tsp chopped sage leaves
a good pinch of ground cinnamon
3 tbsp chopped pecans
sea salt and freshly ground black
   pepper
crushed dried chilli flakes, for
   sprinkling

Preheat the oven to 220°C (200°C fan)/425°F/gas 7. Line a baking tray with baking parchment.

Cut each butternut squash in half lengthways and discard the seeds. Place one half of the squash, cut-side down, on a chopping board and place a spoon or a chopstick on each long side of the squash. This will stop you cutting all the way through it.

With a sharp knife, starting at one end of the squash half, make deep cuts across it horizontally while taking care not to cut right through it. The cuts should be approximately 3mm (⅛ inch) apart. Keep cutting until you reach the other end of the squash, and then repeat with the other halves. Place the squash halves, cut-side up, on the lined baking tray.

Heat the butter, maple syrup and sage in a small pan set over a low heat, stirring until the butter melts and blends with the syrup. Brush some of this glaze over the squash halves and dust with cinnamon. Season lightly with salt and pepper and roast in the preheated oven for 40 minutes, basting 2 to 3 times.

Remove the squash from the oven and sprinkle with the chopped pecans. Drizzle with the remaining butter and maple syrup glaze.

Bake for 20 minutes, or until the squash are cooked, tender and golden brown. Serve immediately, sprinkled with chilli flakes.

VARIATIONS
- Use finely chopped lemon thyme or oregano instead of sage.
- Dust with smoked paprika just before serving.
- Add a dash of balsamic vinegar to the glaze.
- Sprinkle with crumbled feta cheese.

ROAST PUMPKIN AND BLUE CHEESE

//

You can serve this as a tasty side dish or as a first course. Don't worry if you don't have any pumpkin – just substitute butternut squash wedges instead. Vegans can omit the blue cheese or use an artisan plant-based vegan blue cheese, if wished. This is a great way to use up leftover pumpkin or squash, Stilton and nuts.

SERVES 6
PREP 15 MINUTES
COOK 30 MINUTES

1.5kg (3lb 5oz) pumpkin, peeled, deseeded and cut into half-moon wedges
olive oil, for brushing and drizzling
1 tsp sweet paprika
½ tsp freshly grated nutmeg
115g (4oz/scant 1 cup) toasted hazelnuts, roughly crushed
grated zest of ½ lemon
250g (9oz) blue cheese, e.g. Cashel Blue, Stilton
2 red chillies, finely sliced
sea salt and freshly ground black pepper

Preheat the oven to 200°C (180°C fan)/400°F/gas 6.

Lightly brush the pumpkin with oil on both sides and divide them between 2 baking trays, leaving some space in between so they crisp up nicely. Dust with the paprika and nutmeg, and season lightly with salt and pepper.

Roast in the preheated oven for 30 minutes, turning halfway, or until tender inside and crisp on the outside.

Serve the pumpkin, sprinkled with the nuts and lemon zest, and crumble the cheese over the top. Scatter the chilli over the top and serve.

> **TIP:** To toast the hazelnuts, put them in a hot frying pan (skillet) set over a medium to high heat and stir until toasted and fragrant.

VARIATIONS
- Dust the pumpkin with ground cinnamon or ginger.
- Drizzle the pumpkin with 1–2 tablespoons maple syrup before roasting.
- Sprinkle with chopped mint or parsley.
- Use toasted chopped walnuts or pecans.

VEGAN YORKSHIRE PUDDINGS

///

Vegans can make delicious crisp Yorkshires with non-dairy milk plus aquafaba (see note on page 28) to replace the eggs in a traditional Yorkshire batter.

MAKES 12
PREP 10 MINUTES
STAND 15 MINUTES
COOK 20 MINUTES

250g (9oz/2½ cups) self-raising (self-rising) flour
1½ tsp baking powder
½ tsp sea salt
¼ tsp ground turmeric
¼ tsp Dijon mustard (optional)
6 tbsp aquafaba
390ml (13fl oz/generous 1⅓ cups) plant-based milk, e.g. almond
8 tbsp vegetable oil

Preheat the oven to 220°C (200°C fan)/425°F/gas 7.

Sift the flour and baking powder into a bowl and stir in the salt and turmeric. Make a well in the centre.

In a separate bowl, whisk together the mustard, aquafaba and milk. Pour into the well in the dry ingredients and whisk until you have a smooth batter that is bubbly but free from lumps. Set aside to rest for 15 minutes.

Divide the oil into the cups of a 12-hole muffin pan and place on a high shelf in the preheated oven for 10 minutes, or until the oil is sizzling and smoking.

Quickly pour the batter into the cups of the hot pan and return to the oven. Cook for 20 minutes, or until the puddings are well-risen, crisp and golden brown. Do not open the oven door while they are cooking. If you do, they may collapse.

Remove from the oven and serve the Yorkshires immediately.

BUTTERNUT AND BEETROOT WINTER SALAD

///

This naturally sweet and colourful salad is best served warm. It works well for supper, piled on top of some cooked quinoa or couscous. Leave out the feta or replace it with vegan cheese and use Dijon mustard in the dressing, and you'll have a delicious plant-based vegan salad.

SERVES 4
PREP 20 MINUTES
COOK 25–30 MINUTES

500g (1lb 2oz) butternut squash, halved, deseeded and sliced
2 red onions, cut into thin wedges
2 raw beetroots (beets), trimmed, peeled and cut into rounds
olive oil, for drizzling
1 radicchio, trimmed and leaves separated
a handful of wild rocket (arugula)
50g (2oz/scant ½ cup) chopped hazelnuts
a small bunch of flat-leaf parsley, chopped
125g (4oz) feta cheese, crumbled
sea salt and freshly ground black pepper

DRESSING
3 tbsp fruity green olive oil
1 tbsp red wine vinegar
juice of 1 small lemon
a pinch of sugar
1 tsp honey mustard

Preheat the oven to 200°C (180°C fan)/400°F/gas 6. Line 2 baking trays with baking parchment.

Arrange the squash and red onions on one baking tray, and the beetroots on the other. Drizzle with olive oil and season with salt and pepper. Roast in the preheated oven for 25–30 minutes, turning once or twice, or until tender.

Meanwhile, make the dressing: mix all the ingredients together until well blended.

Put the roasted squash and beetroots in a large bowl with the radicchio, rocket and hazelnuts. Toss gently in the dressing. Sprinkle with parsley and check the seasoning.

Divide the salad among 4 serving plates and top with the roasted red onions. Crumble the feta over the top and serve immediately while the salad is still warm.

TIP: For a well-blended salad dressing, put all the ingredients in a screw-top jar and shake vigorously.

VARIATIONS
· Substitute pumpkin for the squash.
· Use red chicory (Belgian endive) instead of radicchio.
· Add some pomegranate seeds or sliced red apples.
· Drizzle with green pesto, tahini or syrupy balsamic vinegar.

MAPLE-GLAZED ROAST CARROTS AND PARSNIPS

//

Carrots and parsnips are naturally sweet and delicious, and adding a citrusy maple syrup glaze for the last few minutes towards the end of the cooking time gives them a fabulous caramelized finish. The perfect accompaniment for your special Christmas Day dinner.

SERVES 6–8
PREP 10 MINUTES
COOK 40 MINUTES

450g (1lb) carrots
450g (1lb) parsnips
2 tbsp olive oil
4 tbsp maple syrup
juice of 1 clementine or tangerine
1 tbsp wholegrain mustard
sea salt and freshly ground black pepper
fresh thyme leaves, to serve

Preheat the oven to 200°C (180°C fan)/400°F/gas 6.

Peel and cut off the ends of the carrots and parsnips. Depending on their size, cut them lengthways into halves or quarters.

Transfer to a roasting pan, drizzle with the olive oil and season with salt and pepper. Cook in the preheated oven, turning once or twice, for 30 minutes.

Put the maple syrup, fruit juice and mustard in a bowl and whisk until well combined.

Pour over the parsnips and carrots and return to the oven for 10 more minutes, or until they are tender inside and crisp, sticky and caramelized on the outside. Serve sprinkled with thyme.

VARIATIONS
- Add some grated clementine zest to the maple syrup mixture.
- Vegetarians can substitute honey for the maple syrup.

TOFU XMAS SALAD

//

In this twist on a classic tricolore salad, we've used crispy golden tofu slices instead of mozzarella to create a colourful red, white and green salad. If you're not a tofu fan, you could substitute griddled or fried sliced vegan halloumi (vegetarians can use regular halloumi).

SERVES 4–6
PREP 15 MINUTES
COOK 4–5 MINUTES

500g (1lb 2oz) firm or extra-firm tofu, pressed (see tip below)
1 tbsp vegetable oil
450g (1lb) large ripe tomatoes, thinly sliced
1 ripe avocado, peeled, stoned (pitted) and thinly sliced
a few basil leaves
sea salt and freshly ground black pepper

DRESSING
1 tbsp olive oil
1 tbsp soy sauce
1 tbsp maple syrup
1 tsp balsamic vinegar
juice of 1 lime

Make the dressing: whisk all the ingredients together in a bowl.

Cut the tofu into slices and season with salt and pepper. Heat the oil in a griddle pan set over a medium to high heat. When the pan is hot, add the tofu and cook for 2–3 minutes until golden, crispy and striped underneath, then turn it over and cook the other side. Remove from the pan and drain on kitchen paper (paper towels).

Arrange the tomatoes, avocado and tofu on a serving platter in attractive overlapping rows or concentric circles. Drizzle with the dressing and scatter the basil leaves over the top. Serve immediately while the tofu is hot.

TIP: Pressing the tofu extracts the water, so it's crispier when cooked. Cut the block into 4–6 slices and place in a single layer between 2 sheets of kitchen paper (paper towels). Cover with a cloth and put some heavy tins on top. Leave for at least 30 minutes and then drain the water.

VARIATIONS
• Add some wild rocket (arugula) or baby spinach leaves.
• Use halved baby plum tomatoes.

VEGAN POMMES DAUPHINOIS

//

This rich and creamy potato dish is always a crowd pleaser and your guests won't believe you when you tell them that it's vegan! You need to use waxy potatoes, such as Desiree, Charlotte or Estima, to get the best results – floury ones like King Edwards or Maris Piper can get too soft and don't keep their shape well.

SERVES 6
PREP 20 MINUTES
COOK 1½ HOURS

vegan butter, for greasing
1kg (2lb 2oz) waxy potatoes (see above), peeled and very thinly sliced
1 onion, finely chopped
3 garlic cloves, crushed
60g (2oz/½ cup) grated vegan cheese
200ml (7fl oz/scant 1 cup) vegan double (heavy) plant-based cream
360ml (12fl oz/1½ cups) plant-based milk, e.g. oat milk
sea salt and freshly ground black pepper

Preheat the oven to 170°C (150°C fan)/325°F/gas 3.

Grease a large shallow ovenproof dish with some vegan butter and add a layer of sliced potatoes. Sprinkle with half the onion, garlic and cheese, and season lightly with salt and pepper. Continue layering up in this way, finishing with a layer of sliced potatoes.

Heat the vegan cream and milk in a saucepan set over a medium heat. Remove from the heat when it's hot (do not allow it to boil) and pour over the layered potatoes.

Cover with foil and bake in the preheated oven for 30 minutes, then remove the foil and bake for 1 hour, or until the potatoes are tender and golden brown on top.

TIP: To make pommes boulangère, substitute 300ml (½ pint/1¼ cups) vegetable stock for the cream and milk and bake for 1½–2 hours, or until the potatoes are tender and the top is golden brown and crisp.

VARIATIONS
· Use a mixture of sliced potatoes and celeriac or parsnips.
· Add some chopped parsley, thyme or rosemary.
· Add a grating of nutmeg to the milk and cream.

SWEET POTATO AND CHESTNUT STUFFING

//

This sweet and savoury stuffing is easy to make and so much healthier and nicer than anything out of a packet. What's more, it's very versatile and you can pick and mix according to your personal tastes and what you've got in your fridge and kitchen cupboards.

SERVES 8
PREP 20 MINUTES
COOK 50–60 MINUTES

900g (2lb) sweet potatoes, peeled and cubed
2 tbsp olive oil, plus extra for drizzling
1 red onion, finely chopped
2 garlic cloves, crushed
leaves stripped from 2 sprigs of thyme
leaves stripped from 2 sprigs of rosemary
a handful of flat-leaf parsley, chopped
200g (7oz/1½ cups) vacuum-packed or cooked chestnuts, roughly chopped
50g (2oz/⅓ cup) dried cranberries
grated zest of 1 lemon
250g (9oz) stale white bread, torn into small pieces
150ml (¼ pint/generous ½ cup) plant-based milk, e.g. oat or almond
sea salt and freshly ground black pepper

Preheat the oven to 200°C (180°C fan)/400°F/gas 6.

Put the sweet potato in a large baking dish and drizzle with a little oil. Season lightly with salt and pepper and bake in the preheated oven for 30–35 minutes, or until just tender and starting to colour.

Meanwhile, heat the remaining oil in a large frying pan (skillet) set over a low heat and cook the onion, stirring occasionally, for 15 minutes until tender but not coloured. Stir in the garlic and herbs and cook for 4–5 minutes. Stir in the chestnuts, cranberries and lemon zest.

Put the bread and milk in a bowl and give it a stir. Leave to soak for 5 minutes, then squeeze out any excess milk, and add to the chestnut mixture.

Spoon the stuffing mixture into the baking dish containing the sweet potato and stir everything gently together. Bake in the oven for 20–25 minutes or until golden brown and crisp.

TIP: You can use any coarse-textured white bread – sourdough and ciabatta are both good.

VARIATIONS
· Stir some chopped nuts into the stuffing before baking: walnuts, hazelnuts or Brazils.
· Add some chopped ready-to-eat apricots or prunes.
· Add some ground cinnamon or grated nutmeg.
· Substitute pumpkin or butternut squash for the sweet potato.

HOLLY JOLLY LEFTOVERS

CHRISTMAS LEFTOVERS FRITTATA

//

Christmas can be very tiring and labour-intensive, so it's often a relief to cook a really simple meal. This festive frittata does the trick and it's a great way of recycling leftover vegetables and cheese. Eat it hot or lukewarm with a crisp salad, or cold the following day.

SERVES 4
PREP 15 MINUTES
COOK 20 MINUTES

2 tbsp olive oil
1 large red onion, chopped
3 garlic cloves, crushed
250g (9oz) leftover roast
  potatoes and/or parsnips, diced
250g (9oz leftover cooked
  Brussels sprouts, kale and/or
  Savoy cabbage, shredded
6 medium free-range eggs
a small handful of parsley,
  chopped
50g (2oz/½ cup) grated Cheddar
  or other hard cheese
cayenne pepper, for dusting
sea salt and freshly ground black
  pepper

Preheat the grill (broiler) on a high setting.

Heat the oil in a medium-sized frying pan (skillet) set over a medium heat. Cook the red onion and garlic, stirring occasionally, for 5 minutes, or until softened. Stir in the leftover vegetables and cook for 5 minutes, stirring occasionally.

Beat the eggs and season lightly with salt and pepper. Stir in the parsley and half of the cheese, and tip into the pan. Fold gently into the vegetables and reduce the heat. Cook gently for about 5 minutes until the frittata is set and golden brown underneath.

Sprinkle the remaining cheese over the top and dust with cayenne. Pop the pan under the hot grill for 3–4 minutes, or until the cheese melts and the frittata is set and golden brown on top.

Slide the frittata out of the pan onto a serving plate and cut into wedges to serve.

VARIATIONS
- Add some red (bell) pepper or spring onions (scallions).
- Add leftover cooked leeks, broccoli, peas, spinach or chestnuts.
- Substitute Stilton, feta or goat's cheese for the Cheddar.
- Serve with cranberry relish, fruity chutney or chilli jam.

ROAST PARSNIP AND BLUE CHEESE SOUP

//

This glorious soup will delight anyone who loves the sweet, earthy flavours of parsnips. If you don't have enough roast parsnips, you can cook some more or just make up the weight with leftover roast sweet potatoes, squash, pumpkin or even regular roast potatoes.

SERVES 4
PREP 15 MINUTES
COOK 25–40 MINUTES

2 tbsp olive oil
1 tbsp butter
2 onions, chopped
2 garlic cloves, crushed
900g (2lb) leftover roast
  parsnips, cut into chunks
1 dessert apple or pear, peeled,
  cored and diced
480ml (16fl oz/2 cups) milk
300ml (½ pint/1¼ cups) hot
  vegetable stock
175g (6oz) Stilton, dolcelatte or
  Cornish Blue cheese, crumbled
sea salt and freshly ground black
  pepper
crisp fried croûtons or snipped
  chives, to serve

Heat the olive oil and butter in a saucepan set over a low to medium heat. Cook the onion, stirring occasionally, for about 10–15 minutes, or until soft, golden and starting to caramelize.

Add the garlic and roast parsnips and cook, stirring occasionally, for 5–10 minutes, or until they are golden brown all over. Add the apple or pear and cook for 4–5 minutes, or until softened.

Bring the milk to the boil in a separate pan and pour over the parsnip mixture. Stir well and then add the hot stock and blue cheese. Purée with a hand-held electric blender, and season to taste with salt and pepper.

Ladle into bowls and serve immediately, topped with crispy croûtons or sprinkled with herbs.

TIP: If you don't have a hand-held blender, use a food processor or blender goblet.

VARIATIONS
• Stir in some crème fraîche or single (light) cream.
• Top with crushed tortilla or vegetable crisps (chips).
• Swirl in some Greek yoghurt before sprinkling with the chives.

THAI LEFTOVER ROAST VEGETABLE CURRY

//

This delicious Thai curry is a good way of transforming leftover vegetables into a colourful and exotic supper. It's so quick and easy and nothing gets wasted. What's more, it will fill your kitchen with wonderfully fragrant and spicy aromas.

SERVES 4
PREP 15 MINUTES
COOK 25 MINUTES

2 tbsp olive oil
1 onion, chopped
3 garlic cloves, crushed
2.5cm (1 inch) piece of fresh root
    ginger, peeled and diced
1 red (bell) pepper, diced
350g (12oz) leftover roast
    potatoes, cubed
350g (12oz) leftover roast
    parsnips, cubed
3–4 tbsp Thai green curry paste
    (see note opposite)
400ml (14fl oz) tin coconut milk
300ml (½ pint/1¼ cups) hot
    vegetable stock
4 lime leaves
200g (7oz) thin green beans,
    trimmed and halved
a handful of coriander (cilantro),
    chopped
juice of 1 lime
1 red bird's eye chilli, shredded
a handful of roasted peanuts
    (optional)
steamed or boiled rice, to serve

Heat the oil in a large saucepan set over a low to medium heat and cook the onion, garlic and ginger, stirring occasionally, for 6–8 minutes, or until tender.

Add the red pepper and roast vegetables and cook for about 5 minutes. Stir in the curry paste and add the coconut milk, vegetable stock, lime leaves and green beans.

Bring to the boil, then reduce the heat to a simmer. Add half of the chopped coriander and cook gently for 10 minutes, or until all the vegetables are tender and the sauce has reduced. Stir in the lime juice and check the seasoning.

Serve, sprinkled with the shredded chilli, roasted peanuts (if using) and the remaining coriander, with some steamed or boiled rice.

NOTE: Use a Thai green curry paste that does not contain any shrimp or fish paste. Check the label before buying or make it yourself.

VARIATIONS
- Stir in some leftover peas, sweet potato or butternut squash.
- Add tomatoes, cubed aubergine (eggplant) or courgettes (zucchini).
- Use Thai basil instead of coriander.
- Serve with rice noodles.

CRISPY HASH WITH POACHED EGGS

//

Nothing gets wasted in this tasty, colourful hash. It's the perfect way to recycle leftover cheese and vegetables for a quick and easy brunch or family meal.

SERVES 4
PREP 10 MINUTES
COOK 12–15 MINUTES

2 tbsp olive oil
1 garlic clove, crushed
1 tsp cumin seeds
½ tsp paprika
900g (2lb) leftover roasted potatoes, parsnips, carrots and/ or swede (rutabaga), cubed
200g (7oz) leftover cooked Brussels sprouts, kale, cabbage and/or greens, shredded
150g (5oz/1 cup) leftover cooked peas
100g (3½oz) Stilton cheese, diced
4 medium free-range eggs
½ tsp crushed dried chilli flakes
sea salt and freshly ground black pepper

Heat the olive oil in a large frying pan (skillet) set over a low to medium heat. Add the garlic and cook for 1 minute without browning. Stir in the cumin seeds and paprika and cook for 1 minute.

Add the leftover vegetables and cook for 10 minutes, stirring occasionally, or until tender and starting to colour and crisp. Season to taste with salt and pepper and stir in the cheese.

Meanwhile, break the eggs into a saucepan of simmering water and poach for 3–4 minutes or until the whites are set and the yolks are still runny. Remove carefully with a slotted spoon and drain on kitchen paper (paper towels).

Divide the hash among 4 serving plates and top each one with a poached egg, sprinkle with chilli flakes and serve immediately.

VARIATIONS
· Add some fried onions or leeks.
· Add some cherry or baby plum tomatoes.
· Add some diced or grated cooked beetroot (beets).
· Fry the eggs instead of poaching them.

CHEESY VEGETABLE TRAYBAKE

//

Don't throw away leftover cooked vegetables, nuts and festive trimmings. They can all be added to a delicious traybake, which is so simple to prepare and cook. And, even better, because everything is cooked in one pan, there's hardly any washing up afterwards!

SERVES 4
PREP 10 MINUTES
COOK 30 MINUTES

900g (2lb) leftover roast potatoes, parsnips, carrots and/ or sweet potatoes

250g (9oz) leftover cooked Brussels sprouts, halved

2 red onions, cut into wedges

2–3 tbsp olive oil

225g (8oz) cheese, e.g. halloumi, Stilton, Cheddar, Brie, goat's cheese or feta

chopped chestnuts, walnuts or pine nuts, for sprinkling

chopped parsley, for sprinkling

cranberry sauce, to serve

sea salt and freshly ground black pepper

Preheat the oven to 200°C (180°C fan)/400°F/gas 6.

Cut the roast vegetables into chunks and place in a large roasting pan with the sprouts and red onions. Drizzle with olive oil and season with salt and pepper.

Bake in the oven for 20 minutes and then crumble, grate or slice the cheese over the top. Sprinkle with the nuts and return to the oven for 10 minutes or until the cheese softens or melts and turns golden.

Serve immediately, sprinkled with parsley, with some cranberry sauce on the side

NOTE: Vegans can use vegan cheese or leave it out and add some cooked or tinned beans, lentils or chickpeas.

VARIATIONS
- Serve with caramelized red onion chutney or quince or crab apple jelly.
- Add some cooked beetroot (beets), butternut squash, cauliflower or broccoli florets.
- Add some leftover stuffing balls or vegetarian sausages for the last 10 minutes.
- Drizzle with pesto or pomegranate molasses.
- Serve with cold bread sauce.

BUBBLE AND SQUEAK BURGERS

//

Serve these delicious vegetable patties as an easy light lunch or supper or prepare them the evening before and chill in the fridge overnight, ready to fry for breakfast or brunch. Vegetarians can add some crumbled Stilton or grated Cheddar.

SERVES 4
PREP 15 MINUTES
COOK 20 MINUTES

4 tbsp olive oil
2 onions, finely chopped
3 garlic cloves, crushed
¼ tsp crushed dried chilli flakes
500g (1lb 2oz) leftover cooked potatoes, parsnips and/or carrots
300g (10oz) leftover cooked Brussels sprouts and/or green cabbage
plain (all-purpose) flour, for dusting
sea salt and freshly ground black pepper
cranberry relish, to serve

Heat 2 tablespoons of the oil in a large frying pan (skillet) set over a medium heat. Cook the onion and garlic, stirring occasionally, for 8–10 minutes, or until softened and golden. Stir in the chilli flakes and season with salt and pepper.

Meanwhile, pulse all the leftover vegetables in a food processor until you have a coarsely chopped mixture that clings together. Add to the onion in the pan and stir well.

Transfer to a bowl and briefly set aside until the mixture is cool enough to handle. Divide into 8 small or 4 large portions. Using your hands, mould each one into a patty (burger) and dust lightly with flour.

Heat the remaining oil in a large non-stick frying pan set over a medium heat and cook the burgers for 4–5 minutes each side, or until heated right through and crisp and golden brown. Serve hot with cranberry relish and some salad or coleslaw.

> **TIP:** Instead of making individual burgers, you can cook the bubble and squeak as one large 'cake' and serve it cut into wedges.

VARIATIONS
• Add some ground cumin, turmeric and garam masala.
• Cook some grated fresh root ginger with the onions and garlic.
• Serve with cranberry sauce or spicy mango chutney.

TEATIME
TREATS

CHOCOLATE YULE LOG

///

This is more like a chocolate roulade than an everyday Swiss roll. It's rich and moist, perfect served sliced for tea or as a dessert over the Christmas holidays. If wished, you can decorate it with sprigs of holly or miniature Christmas tree, Santa and reindeer cake decorations.

SERVES 8
PREP 20 MINUTES
COOK 15–20 MINUTES

oil, for brushing
175g (6oz) dark (bittersweet)
    chocolate (70% cocoa solids)
2 tbsp hot water
5 medium free-range eggs,
    separated
175g (6oz/¾ cup) caster
    (superfine) sugar
icing (confectioner's) sugar, for
    dusting
300ml (½ pint/1¼ cups) double
    (heavy) cream
grated zest of 1 orange
2 knobs of stem ginger in syrup,
    drained and diced (optional)

VARIATIONS
- Add some Cointreau or Grand Marnier to the whipped cream.
- Serve with fresh raspberries or strawberries.
- Decorate with edible glitter, chocolate holly leaves or gold stars.

Preheat the oven to 180°C (160°C fan)/350°F/gas 4. Lightly brush a 34 x 23cm (14 x 9 inch) shallow Swiss roll tin (jelly roll pan) with oil and line with baking parchment so it comes up the sides of the tin.

Break the chocolate into pieces and place in a heatproof bowl. Bring a small pan of water to the boil and remove from the heat. Place the bowl of chocolate over the pan without touching the water below. Stir occasionally with a flat-bladed knife until the chocolate softens and melts. Add the hot water and stir gently.

In a bowl, using a hand-held electric whisk, beat the egg yolks and sugar until pale, thick and creamy. Stir in the melted chocolate until well blended.

In a clean, dry bowl, beat the egg whites until they form stiff peaks. Stir a spoonful into the chocolate mixture to slacken it and then gently fold in the remainder in a figure-of-eight motion with a metal spoon.

Transfer to the lined tin and level the top with a palette knife. Bake in the preheated oven for 15–20 minutes or until risen, springy and firm on top.

Carefully slide the roulade on the baking parchment out of the tin and onto a wire rack. Cover with a clean tea towel dampened with water and leave until cold.

When you're ready to fill the roulade, place a large sheet of baking parchment on a work surface and sift some icing sugar over it. Place the cold sponge, baking parchment-side up, on top of the icing sugar, and then carefully peel off the backing paper.

Beat the cream in a food mixer, or use a hand-held electric whisk, until it holds its shape. Take care not to overbeat – it shouldn't be too stiff. Stir in the orange zest and ginger (if using) and spread evenly over the roulade, leaving a border of 1cm (½ inch) around the edges.

Using the paper to help you, roll up the roulade like a Swiss roll from one short end. It may crack a little but don't worry about that. Transfer to a serving plate with the join underneath, then dust with more icing sugar and decorate, if wished, with holly or Christmas cake decorations.

Serve cut into slices. It will keep well in an airtight container in the fridge for 2 days.

SNOWY VEGAN SALTED CARAMEL CUPCAKES

//

These fabulous cupcakes are easy to make and totally irresistible with their creamy coconut topping. Unless you tell them, nobody will ever guess that they are vegan and dairy-free.

MAKES 12 CUPCAKES
PREP 30 MINUTES
COOK 20–25 MINUTES

240ml (8fl oz/1 cup) plant-based milk, e.g. almond or soy, at room temperature
1 tsp apple cider vinegar
175g (6oz/1¾ cups) self-raising (self-rising) flour
1½ tsp baking powder
½ tsp sea salt
175g (6oz/¾ cup) caster (superfine) sugar
75ml (2½fl oz/5 tbsp) sunflower or avocado oil
2 tsp vanilla extract
12 tsp vegan salted caramel sauce

CREAMY COCONUT TOPPING
400ml (14fl oz) tin full-fat coconut milk
150g (5oz/generous 1 cup) icing (confectioner's) sugar
½ tsp vanilla extract
75g (3oz/1 cup) desiccated (shredded) coconut

VARIATION
• For children, top the cakes with miniature Christmas tree or polar bear cake decorations.

The day before you make the cupcakes, place the tin of coconut milk for the topping in the fridge and leave overnight.

Preheat the oven to 180°C (160°C fan)/350°F/gas 4. Place 12 paper cases (liners) in a 12-hole muffin pan.

Put the milk and vinegar in a bowl and set aside for 5 minutes, or until the milk curdles and thickens.

Sift the flour, baking powder and salt into a mixing bowl and stir in the sugar until well combined.

Add the curdled milk, oil and vanilla and beat with a hand-held electric whisk until you have a smooth mixture free of lumps.

Divide the mixture among the paper cases and bake in the preheated oven for 20–25 minutes, or until well risen and golden brown. Leave the cupcakes to cool on a wire rack, then cut a shallow inverted cone piece out of the centre of each cake. Place a spoonful of salted caramel sauce in each hole and then replace the cones.

Make the coconut topping: open the chilled coconut milk tin upside down and drain off the thin liquid. Transfer the thick coconut milk to a mixing bowl and, using a hand-held electric whisk, beat with the icing sugar and vanilla until well combined and fluffy.

Spread the coconut topping thickly over the cupcakes and then sprinkle generously with the coconut. Store in an airtight container in the fridge for up to 2 days.

CHRISTMAS CINNAMON SHORTBREAD

///

For many of us, Christmas is not complete without some buttery, melt-in-the-mouth shortbread. Why not make double the quantity and wrap the shortbread biscuits (cookies) in pretty packaging and ribbons for delicious edible gifts

SERVES 8
PREP 35 MINUTES
FREEZE 6+ HOURS

200g (7oz/2 cups) plain (all-purpose) flour
100g (3½oz/⅔ cup) rice flour
100g (3½oz/scant ½ cup) caster (superfine) sugar, plus extra for sprinkling
200g (7oz/scant 1 cup) butter, diced, plus extra for greasing
1 tsp ground cinnamon, plus extra for sprinkling
grated zest of 1 orange

Preheat the oven to 180°C (160°C fan)/350°F/gas 4. Lightly butter a 20 x 20cm (8 x 8 inch) cake tin.

Mix the flour, rice flour and sugar in a large bowl. Add the butter and rub together with your fingertips until the mixture resembles fine breadcrumbs. Stir in the cinnamon and orange zest.

Knead gently to bring everything together to form a soft dough. Transfer to a bowl or work surface and work with your hands into a smooth ball of dough.

Transfer to the buttered cake tin and press the mixture down firmly, levelling the top. Prick several times with a fork and then bake in the preheated oven for 20–25 minutes or until pale golden.

Set aside to cool in the tin before cutting into squares. Mix a little caster sugar with a large pinch of cinnamon and sprinkle over the shortbread. Store in an airtight container for up to 2 weeks.

TIP: You can blitz the butter and sugar for the shortbread in a food processor, then add the flours and pulse until the mixture resembles breadcrumbs.

VARIATIONS
· Add some chocolate chips to the shortbread mixture.
· Add some chopped lavender or rosemary leaves.
· Roll out the shortbread dough between sheets of baking parchment and cut into shapes using Christmas cutters (Xmas trees, etc.).

DATE AND BANANA CHRISTMAS MUFFINS

//

These vegan muffins are perfect for a light breakfast when you're in a hurry and need to grab a bite to eat, or a delicious snack at any time of the day. Fresh Medjool dates are usually widely available at Christmas. Always use them in preference to dried dates.

MAKES 12
PREP 15 MINUTES
COOK 20–25 MINUTES

225g (8oz/2¼ cups) self-raising (self-rising) flour
a pinch of fine sea salt
150g (5oz/⅔ cup) soft light brown sugar
2 ripe bananas, mashed
120ml (4fl oz/½ cup) sunflower oil, plus extra for brushing
1 tsp orange flower water
grated zest and juice of 2 satsumas or clementines
150ml (¼ pint/generous ½ cup) almond milk
1 tsp bicarbonate of soda (baking soda)
1 tsp apple cider vinegar
6 Medjool dates, stoned (pitted) and chopped
4 tbsp sesame seeds

Preheat the oven to 180°C (160°C fan)/350°F/gas 4. Line a 12-hole muffin pan with paper cases (liners).

Put the flour, salt and sugar in a large bowl and stir well. Make a well in the centre and add the mashed bananas, oil, orange flower water and citrus zest and juice.

Whisk the milk, bicarbonate of soda and vinegar together in a bowl and pour into the well. Stir gently until everything is well combined. Fold in the dates, distributing them evenly throughout the mixture (batter).

Divide the mixture among the paper cases and sprinkle the sesame seeds over the top. Bake for 20–25 minutes or until well-risen, golden brown and a thin skewer comes out clean when inserted into the middle of a muffin.

Leave in the muffin pan for 5 minutes and then transfer the muffins to a wire rack to cool. Store in an airtight container and eat within 2 days.

VARIATIONS
• Add a few drops of vanilla extract.
• Dust with icing (confectioner's) sugar.
• Add some chopped nuts, e.g. walnuts, pecans or hazelnuts.

VEGAN MINCE PIES WITH BRANDY BUTTER

//

Use a jar of readymade vegan mincemeat to make these delicious pies, which are served with homemade brandy butter. They also make lovely Christmas gifts.

MAKES 12
PREP 20 MINUTES
CHILL 30 MINUTES
COOK 20 MINUTES

250g (9oz/2½ cups) plain (all-purpose) flour
¼ tsp sea salt
150g (5oz/generous ½ cup) vegan butter, diced, plus extra for greasing
2 tbsp caster (superfine) sugar
2–3 tbsp ice-cold water
375g (13oz/1⅔ cups) vegan mincemeat
plant-based milk, for brushing
icing (confectioner's) sugar, for dusting

BRANDY BUTTER
200g (7oz/scant 1 cup) vegan butter, softened
200g (7oz/scant 1½ cups) icing (confectioner's) sugar
3 tbsp vegan-friendly brandy

TIP: If the brandy butter curdles, just add more icing sugar and beat until smooth.

Preheat the oven to 200°C (180°C fan)/400°F/gas 6. Grease a 12-hole tartlet tin (pan) with vegan butter.

Make the pastry (pie crust): sift the flour and salt into a large bowl. Add the vegan butter and, using your fingers, rub it into the flour until the mixture resembles coarse breadcrumbs. Stir in the sugar and then mix in the water to form a soft ball of dough. Place in a polythene bag and chill in the fridge for 30 minutes.

Roll out the pastry about 3mm (⅛ inch) thick on a lightly floured surface and cut out 12 rounds with an 8cm (3 inch) pastry cutter. Use to line the greased pan. Fill the pies with mincemeat, almost up to the top.

Re-roll the leftover pastry and trimmings and, using a 6cm (2 inch) star-shaped pastry cutter, cut out 12 stars to top the pies.Lightly brush the top of each pie with milk and bake for about 20 minutes, or until the pastry is crisp and golden.

Meanwhile, make the brandy butter: beat the butter with a wooden spoon in a bowl. Beat in the icing sugar, a little at a time. Gradually add the brandy. Whisk with a hand-held electric whisk or in a food mixer until the butter is light and fluffy. Transfer to a container, then cover and chill in the fridge overnight.

Leave the pies to cool for 10 minutes, before running a knife around them and carefully removing them from the tin. Cool on a wire rack and dust with icing sugar. When cold, store in an airtight container for up to 5 days.

Serve the pies hot, warm or even cold with the brandy butter.

VARIATION
• Add grated clementine or orange zest to the pastry.

STICKY CLEMENTINE DRIZZLE CAKE

//

This is one of the simplest cakes you'll ever make. It's wonderfully light and moist (due to the ground almonds) and has a clean, sharp citrusy flavour – the perfect antidote to all that rich and creamy festive food. We've just drizzled ours with syrup but you could pour some glacé icing (frosting) over the top and sprinkle with flaked almonds or candied peel to make it look pretty.

SERVES 10–12
PREP 20 MINUTES
COOK 1–1¼ HOURS

225g (8oz/1 cup) butter, softened, plus extra for greasing
225g (8oz/1 cup) golden caster (superfine) sugar
4 large free-range eggs
115g (4oz/1 cup) plain (all-purpose) flour, sifted
1 tsp baking powder
115g (4oz/¾ cup) ground almonds (almond flour)
grated zest and juice of 2 clementines

SYRUP
juice of 2 clementines
4 tbsp caster (superfine) sugar

Preheat the oven to 170°C (150°C fan)/325°F/gas 3. Butter a 20cm (8 inch) round springform cake tin (pan) and line the base and sides with baking parchment.

In a food mixer or using a hand-held electric whisk, beat the butter and sugar until pale, creamy and fluffy. Add the eggs, one at a time, beating well between each addition. Add a tablespoon of sifted flour with the last 2 eggs to prevent the mixture curdling.

Add the sifted flour and baking powder and beat well, then beat in the ground almonds. Stir in the clementine zest and juice. If the mixture is too thick, slacken it with 1–2 tablespoons milk.

Pour into the tin and bake for 1–1¼ hours or until the cake is well risen and a thin skewer inserted into the centre comes out clean. Leave in the cake tin to cool while you make the syrup.

Heat the clementine juice and sugar in a pan set over a medium heat. Stir gently until the sugar dissolves.

Pierce the warm cake several times with a skewer and drizzle the hot syrup over the top. Leave the cake to cool in the tin before turning out and removing the lining paper.

Store in an airtight container for up to 5 days. Serve cut into slices for tea or a snack, or with crème fraîche as a dessert.

VARIATIONS
- Use oranges, mandarins, tangerines or satsumas instead of clementines.
- For a sharper, more refreshing taste, use lemons or limes.

VEGAN CHRISTMAS CAKE

//

This boozy cake must be made several weeks in advance to give you time to 'feed' the cake with brandy and to marzipan and ice it ready to cut on Christmas Day. You will also need to prepare and soak the dried fruit the day before you bake the cake.

SERVES 12
SOAK OVERNIGHT
PREP 1 HOUR
COOK 2–3 HOURS

350g (12oz/2½ cups) mixed dried fruit, e.g. raisins, currants, sultanas

100g (3½oz/1 cup) mixed candied peel

100g (3½oz/⅔ cup) dried cranberries

100g (3½oz/1 cup) glacé cherries, halved

120ml (4fl oz/½ cup) vegan-friendly brandy

200g (7oz/scant 1 cup) vegan butter, softened, plus extra for greasing

200g (7oz/1 cup) soft light brown sugar

2 tbsp black treacle (blackstrap molasses)

grated zest of 1 orange

grated zest of 1 lemon

325g (11½oz/3¼ cups) plain (all-purpose) flour, sifted

½ tsp baking powder

100g (3½oz/⅔ cup) ground almonds (almond flour)

One day ahead of making the cake, put all the dried fruit, candied peel, cranberries and cherries in a large bowl with the brandy. Mix well and then cover the bowl and leave to soak overnight.

The following day, preheat the oven to 150°C (130°C fan)/300°F/gas 2. Butter a deep 20cm (8 inch) cake tin (pan) and line with double thickness baking parchment. Use kitchen string to tie a double layer of newspaper around the outside of the tin.

In a food mixer or using a hand-held electric whisk, beat the butter and sugar until soft, pale and fluffy. Beat in the black treacle and orange and lemon zest.

On a low speed, mix in the flour, baking powder, ground almonds, bicarbonate of soda and spices, a little at a time. Beat in the milk and lemon juice, then fold in the almonds and the soaked dried fruit plus the soaking liquid. Add some more milk to slacken the mixture if it seems too thick and dry.

Spoon the mixture into the lined tin and level the top. Bake in the preheated oven for 2–3 hours, or until the cake is cooked. Check by inserting a thin skewer into the centre – it's ready when it comes out clean. Leave the cake to cool in the tin and then turn out onto a wire rack.

When the cake is cold, make some holes in the top with a skewer or a toothpick and sprinkle with 1–2 tablespoons brandy. Wrap the cake in baking parchment and then in kitchen foil and store in an airtight tin. Unwrap it once every 2 weeks and 'feed' with more brandy in the same way. Stop feeding it a week before you intend to ice it.

1 tsp bicarbonate of soda (baking soda)

2 tsp mixed spice (apple pie spice)

1 tsp ground cinnamon

½ tsp ground nutmeg

120ml (4fl oz/½ cup) plant-based milk

juice of 1 small lemon

50g (2oz/⅔ cup) chopped or flaked almonds

FOR FEEDING AND ICING THE CAKE

vegan-friendly brandy, for feeding the cake (see note)

2 tbsp apricot jam

500g (1lb 2oz) vegan marzipan

icing (confectioner's) sugar, for dusting

800g (1lb 12oz) vegan ready-to-roll fondant icing

When you're ready to cover the cake, warm the apricot jam in a pan set over a low heat. Brush the warm jam over the top and sides of the cake.

Roll out one-third of the marzipan 1cm (½ inch) thick on a work surface dusted with icing sugar and cut out a 20cm (8 inch) circle. Roll out the remaining marzipan and use to cover the sides of the cake, pressing it firmly onto the jam to help it stick. Place the marzipan circle on top.

To ice the cake, roll out the fondant icing in a large circle and drape it over the cake. Smooth the top with an icing smoother, and gently pull the icing down the sides of the cake. Run your hand around the sides to smooth it and help the icing to stick and then smooth with the icing smoother. Trim away the excess icing at the base.

Decorate the top with Christmas cake decorations and tie a broad decorative ribbon around the sides.

NOTE: Allow several weeks (up to 3 months) for 'feeding' the cake if you want it to be really moist and strongly infused with brandy. You will need to add 1–2 tablespoons once every 2 weeks and then leave it for a week to dry out before covering with marzipan (almond paste) and icing.

TIP: When covering with marzipan and icing the cake, work quickly before they dry out.

VARIATIONS
- Use vegan-friendly dark rum, sherry or whisky instead of brandy.
- Substitute orange juice for alcohol when soaking the dried fruit.
- Make vegan royal icing with aquafaba replacing the egg whites.

LEBKUCHEN STARS

//

These spicy gingerbread cookies are traditional sweet treats in Germany during the Christmas holiday season. They are wonderfully aromatic and their fragrance will permeate your kitchen while they are cooking. Serve them with coffee or at the end of a meal.

MAKES ABOUT 30 COOKIES
PREP 30 MINUTES
COOK 12 MINUTES

85g (3oz/⅓ cup) unsalted butter
100ml (3½fl oz/scant ½ cup) clear honey
100ml (3½fl oz/scant ½ cup) black treacle (blackstrap molasses)
2 tbsp dark muscovado sugar
finely grated zest of 1 lemon
250g (9oz/2½ cups) self-raising (self-rising) flour, plus extra for rolling
¼ tsp sea salt
½ tsp bicarbonate of soda (baking soda)
2 tsp ground cinnamon
1 tsp ground ginger
½ tsp ground allspice
¼ tsp ground cloves
50g (2oz/⅓ cup) ground almonds (almond flour)
1 medium free-range egg yolk

LEMON ICING
150g (5oz/generous 1 cup) icing (confectioner's) sugar
juice of 1 lemon

Preheat the oven to 180°C (160°C fan)/350°F/gas 4. Line 2 large baking trays with baking parchment.

Put the butter, honey, black treacle, sugar and lemon zest in a large saucepan and set over a medium heat. Stir to combine and when it melts, remove from the heat and set aside.

After 5 minutes, sift in the flour, salt, bicarbonate of soda and spices and stir well. Gently fold in the ground almonds and egg yolk until you have a soft, smooth and oily dough.

On a floured work surface, knead the dough lightly until smooth and then roll it out to a thickness of 1cm (½ inch). Cut the dough into stars with a star-shaped pastry cutter and place them on the lined baking trays. Roll out any leftover dough and cut some more.

Bake in the preheated oven for 12 minutes until lightly browned, then leave to cool on the trays for 10 minutes before transferring the cookies to a wire rack.

When the cookies are cold, make the icing: mix the icing sugar and lemon juice in a bowl. If it's too thick, add a little more lemon juice. Dip the top of each cookie into the icing, then transfer to the wire rack and leave until the icing sets. Store in an airtight container for up to 2 weeks.

VARIATIONS
· Dip the cold cookies in melted dark (bittersweet) chocolate.
· Add a tablespoon of cocoa powder to the cookie mixture.
· Add some grated orange zest or vanilla extract.
· Add some diced candied lemon, orange or citrus peel.
· Add some ground nutmeg and cardamom.

DAZZLING
DESSERTS

JEWELLED VEGAN PAVLOVA

//

You only need the drained liquid from one tin of chickpeas to make a vegan pavlova. It's a great dessert for festive entertaining and parties and your guests will be surprised when you tell them it's made with chickpea brine, not eggs!

SERVES 6–8
PREP 25 MINUTES
COOK 1½ –2 HOURS
COOL 45 MINUTES

120ml (4fl oz/½ cup) aquafaba
  – liquid from 400g (14oz) tin
  chickpeas (garbanzos)
225g (8oz/1 cup) caster
  (superfine) sugar
1 tbsp cornflour (cornstarch)
1 tsp apple cider vinegar

TOPPING
200ml (7fl oz/scant 1 cup) tinned
  coconut cream
200g (7oz/scant 1 cup) coconut
  dairy-free yoghurt
1 tsp vanilla extract
1 tbsp maple syrup
3 tbsp coarsely grated dark plain
  (semisweet) chocolate
seeds of 1 pomegranate

VARIATIONS
- Flavour the meringue with grated lemon or orange zest or vanilla.
- Top with passionfruit, kiwi fruit or mango.
- Sprinkle with toasted flaked almonds.

The day before you plan to make the pavlova, place the tin of coconut cream and the yoghurt in the fridge and chill overnight.

Preheat the oven to 140°C (120°C fan)/275°F/gas 1. Trace a 23cm (9 inch) circle on a sheet of baking parchment and use to line a baking tray.

Pour the aquafaba into the bowl of an electric mixer (or a deep mixing bowl if using a hand-held whisk). Whip the aquafaba for 3–5 minutes until fluffy and soft peaks form. Start on a slow speed and gradually increase it to high.

Mix the sugar and cornflour in a small bowl and then start adding it, 2 tablespoons at a time, to the aquafaba, whisking on a high speed until all the sugar has been added. Add the vinegar and keep whisking until the meringue is glossy with stiff peaks. You'll know when the meringue is ready because when you lift the beaters out, the meringue will stay in place and not drop off.

Spoon the meringue onto the marked-out circle on the baking parchment, spreading it out to the edges and making a slight hollow in the centre. Place in the preheated oven and reduce the heat to 130°C (110°C fan)/250°F/gas ½. Bake for 1½–2 hours, or until the pavlova is crisp on the outside and dry on top. Turn off the oven, open the door slightly so it's ajar, and leave the meringue inside for 45 minutes, or until cool.

Just before serving the pavlova, whip the chilled coconut cream in a food mixer or with a hand-held electric whisk until it forms stiff peaks and holds its shape. On a low speed, beat in the yoghurt, vanilla and maple syrup.

Spread the coconut cream topping over the meringue. Sprinkle with the grated chocolate and pomegranate seeds and serve cut into slices.

PANNA COTTA WITH CRANBERRY COULIS

///

In Italian, *panna cotta* literally means 'cooked cream'. These quivering little creamy desserts look very elegant and are served in a colourful pool of sieved cranberries. If preferred, you can drizzle the coulis over the top of the panna cottas.

SERVES 6
PREP 20 MINUTES
COOK 20 MINUTES
CHILL 3+ HOURS

1 vanilla pod (bean)
300ml (½ pint/1¼ cups) double (heavy) cream
300ml (½ pint/1¼ cups) milk
2 tsp agar agar powder
6 tbsp caster (superfine) sugar

CRANBERRY COULIS
200g (7oz/2 cups) fresh cranberries
100g (3½oz/scant ½ cup) caster (superfine) sugar
grated zest of 1 orange
4 tbsp orange juice

VARIATIONS
- Instead of a vanilla bean, use a few drops of vanilla extract.
- Decorate with a few whole cranberries.
- Serve with a raspberry coulis instead.

With a sharp knife, slice open the vanilla pod lengthways from end to end and scrape out the seeds. Set aside.

Place the vanilla pod and seeds in a pan with the cream and milk. Add the agar agar and whisk well. Leave to stand for 15 minutes.

Add the sugar and set the pan over a medium heat. Stir until the sugar and agar agar dissolve and, when the mixture is very hot and nearly at boiling point, reduce the heat to low and cook for 3 minutes.

Turn off the heat and remove the vanilla pod (don't discard it, see tip opposite). Strain the mixture through a sieve into a jug.

Pour the mixture into 6 dariole moulds (molds) or 6cm (2½ inch) ramekins, then cover and chill in the fridge for at least 3 hours, or until the panna cotta sets. Don't worry if it's not super firm – it should be a soft set with the slightest hint of a wobble.

Meanwhile, make the cranberry coulis: put all the ingredients in a saucepan and set over a medium heat. Stir until the sugar dissolves and then increase the heat and bring to the boil. Reduce the heat to low and simmer gently for 15 minutes, or until the berries burst. Pass the mixture through a fine sieve, pressing it down with a spoon, into a bowl and leave until cold. Discard the cranberry solids in the sieve.

Unmould the panna cottas onto 6 serving plates. Carefully run a thin knife around the edge of the ramekins or moulds and invert them onto the plates. If the panna cotta doesn't drop out, quickly dip the moulds or ramekins into a bowl of hot water and try again. Pour the cranberry coulis around each panna cotta so it sits in a pretty scarlet pool. Serve immediately.

TIP: Don't throw away the used vanilla pod. Wash and dry it thoroughly and then pop it into a jar of sugar. Cover with the lid and leave for the vanilla flavour to infuse the sugar.

PROFITEROLE CHRISTMAS TREE

//

Everyone loves profiteroles and this fail-safe recipe is surprisingly easy. For a festive touch, you could pile them up in the shape of a Christmas tree and drizzle them with chocolate sauce. You could go the whole hog and decorate them with edible golden stars, sprinkles or glitter for a really impressive centrepiece.

SERVES 6
PREP 40 MINUTES
COOK 20–25 MINUTES

85g (3oz/⅓ cup) butter, cubed
200ml (7fl oz/scant 1 cup) water
100g (3½oz/1 cup) plain (all-purpose) flour, sifted
a pinch of sea salt
3 medium free-range eggs
clear honey, for dipping and stacking
icing (confectioner's) sugar, for dusting

Preheat the oven to 200°C (180°C fan)/400°F/gas 6. Line a baking tray with baking parchment.

Put the butter and water in a saucepan and set over a medium heat. When the butter melts, increase the heat and bring to the boil.

Add the flour and salt and immediately take the pan off the heat. Beat until the mixture is thick and smooth and forms a ball that leaves the sides of the pan clean. Set aside to cool for 5 minutes and then beat in the eggs, one at a time, beating well between additions until the choux pastry is glossy and smooth.

Drop spoonfuls of the mixture onto the lined baking tray, leaving plenty of space around them. Bake in the preheated oven for 20–25 minutes until well risen, puffy and golden brown. Transfer to a wire rack and leave to cool.

Make the salted caramel cream: heat the butter, muscovado sugar, golden syrup and salt in a saucepan set over a low heat, stirring until the sugar dissolves. Remove from the heat and leave to cool.

Meanwhile, whip the cream until it stands in soft peaks and then beat in the icing sugar. Add the cooled salted caramel mixture and fold in gently. Use to fill a piping bag fitted with a medium nozzle. Make a hole in each profiterole with a skewer and pipe in the cream.

SALTED CARAMEL CREAM

50g (2oz/¼ cup) butter

2 tbsp muscovado sugar

2 tbsp golden (corn) syrup

½ tsp sea salt flakes

400ml (14fl oz/generous 1½ cups) double (heavy) cream

1 tbsp icing (confectioner's) sugar, sifted

CHOCOLATE SAUCE

85g (3oz) dark (bittersweet) chocolate, cut into squares

100ml (3½fl oz/scant ½ cup) double (heavy) cream

Make the chocolate sauce: bring a small pan of water to the boil and remove from the heat. Put the chocolate in a heatproof bowl and suspend it over the pan without touching the water below. Stir occasionally with a flat-bladed knife until the chocolate melts, then gradually stir in the cream. Leave for a few minutes to firm up to a coating consistency.

Pile up the profiteroles on a large serving plate in a cone shape like a Christmas tree. Start with a wide circle at the bottom and progressively smaller layers on top. Secure them in place by dipping the base of each profiterole in honey to help them stick. Lightly dust with icing sugar and drizzle the chocolate sauce over the top.

VARIATIONS
- Use white chocolate to make the sauce, so it looks like snow.
- Use light soft brown sugar instead of muscovado in the filling.
- Drizzle with salted caramel sauce.

VARIATIONS

- Sandwich the sponge slices with raspberry or cherry jam (jelly).
- If you can't get fresh raspberries, use frozen ones.
- Top with pomegranate seeds.
- Instead of limoncello, sprinkle with Grand Marnier or sweet sherry.
- Use plant-based whipping cream for the topping.

VEGAN XMAS TRIFLE

//

We've made the sponge and creamy topping for this trifle but if you don't have time to cook, you could buy ready-made ones instead. For those of you who don't like Christmas pudding, this is the perfect dessert for your Christmas Day lunch or dinner.

SERVES 6–8
PREP 30 MINUTES
COOK 30 MINUTES
CHILL 3½ HOURS

200ml (7fl oz/scant 1 cup) tinned coconut cream
200g (7oz/scant 1 cup) coconut dairy-free yoghurt
3 tbsp vegan lemon curd
4 tbsp limoncello
300g (10oz) raspberries
500ml (17fl oz/generous 2 cups) vegan vanilla custard
1 tsp vanilla extract
1 tbsp maple syrup
3 tbsp toasted flaked almonds, for sprinkling
zest of 1 lemon, sliced into thin shreds

SPONGE
150g (5oz/generous ½ cup) caster (superfine) sugar
200g (7oz/2 cups) self-raising (self-rising) flour, sifted
1 tsp baking powder
100g (3½oz/scant ½ cup) vegan butter, melted
200ml (7fl oz/scant 1 cup) dairy-free unsweetened milk
1 tsp vanilla extract

The day before, place the tin of coconut cream and the yoghurt in the fridge and leave to chill overnight.

Preheat the oven to 180°C (160°C fan)/350°F/gas 4. Oil and line a 20cm (8 inch) round cake tin (pan) with baking parchment.

Make the sponge: put the sugar, flour and baking powder in a large bowl and mix together. In another bowl, mix the melted butter, milk and vanilla extract. Pour into the dry ingredients and beat until well combined.

Spoon the mixture into the cake tin and bake for 30 minutes, or until risen and a skewer comes out clean. Leave to cool in the tin for 10 minutes and then turn out onto a wire rack.

When the sponge is cold, peel off the backing paper and cut into 8 slices. Cut each one in half horizontally and spread 8 of them with lemon curd. Sandwich together with the remaining halves and place them in a large glass serving bowl, fitting them in tightly. Sprinkle with the limoncello and set aside for 10 minutes, so the sponge can absorb it.

Cover the sponge with the raspberries, reserving a few for decoration, and then pour the vanilla custard over the top. Chill in the fridge for 30 minutes to firm up the custard.

Whip the chilled coconut cream in a food mixer or with a hand-held electric whisk until it forms stiff peaks and holds its shape. On a low speed, beat in the yoghurt, vanilla and maple syrup. Spread it over the top of the custard and chill in the fridge for at least 3 hours.

Sprinkle the almonds, lemon zest and reserved raspberries over the trifle just before serving.

BAKED PANETTONE PUDDING

//

Panettone is a sweet, moist and buttery textured bread, studded with raisins, orange and citrus peel, which is served all over Italy at Christmas. For this dessert, you need to use the original fruit panettone (classico) rather than the flavoured ones (limoncello, chocolate, pistachio cream, etc.).

SERVES 6–8
PREP 20 MINUTES
STAND 20–25 MINUTES
COOK 40–45 MINUTES

butter, for greasing
500g (1lb 2oz) fruit panettone,
  thinly sliced
50g (2oz/¼ cup) sultanas (golden
  raisins), soaked in hot water
  and drained
3 tbsp candied peel
grated zest of 1 orange
icing (confectioner's) sugar,
  for dusting
pouring cream or ice cream,
  to serve

CUSTARD
4 medium free-range eggs
50g (2oz/¼ cup) caster
  (superfine) sugar
300ml (½ pint/1¼ cups) double
  (heavy) cream
300ml (½ pint/1¼ cups) full-fat
  milk

> **TIP:** Soaking the sultanas first in hot water plumps them up.

Preheat the oven to 180°C (160°C fan)/350°F/gas 4. Butter a 2-litre (2-quart) ovenproof dish.

Make the custard: beat the eggs and sugar in a bowl until combined. Heat the cream and milk in a saucepan set over a high heat and just before it comes to the boil, remove from the heat and pour it over the beaten eggs. Stir well until combined.

Cut the panettone slices into triangles and place them, overlapping each other, in the buttered dish. Scatter with the sultanas and candied peel and sprinkle the orange zest on top.

Pour the hot custard over the top to soak the panettone. Set aside for 10–15 minutes.

Place the dish in a roasting pan half-filled with cold water and bake in the preheated oven for 40–45 minutes, or until golden brown on top and the custard is set but still slightly wobbly.

Set aside for 10 minutes before serving, dusted with icing sugar, with pouring cream or ice cream.

VARIATIONS
- For a richer, more luxurious pudding, lightly butter the panettone slices.
- Add some dark chocolate chunks or chips before baking.
- Add some dark orange marmalade with the sultanas.
- Use dried cranberries instead of sultanas.
- Add a few drops of vanilla extract to the custard.

CHRISTMAS COMPÔTE WITH COCONUT YOGHURT

//

You can serve this spiced pear and dried fruit compôte for breakfast as well as a dessert.
It will keep well in a covered container in the fridge for up to 3 days.

SERVES 6
PREP 10 MINUTES
COOK 25 MINUTES
CHILL OVERNIGHT (OPTIONAL)

3 pears, peeled, cut into quarters
    and cored
300ml (½ pint/1¼ cups) water
50g (2oz/¼ cup) golden
    (unrefined) granulated sugar
grated zest and juice of 1 orange
1 cinnamon stick
3 whole cloves
4 cardamom pods, split
1 star anise
225g (8oz/2 cups) mixed dried
    fruit, e.g. diced apricots, apples,
    peaches, figs, cranberries
coconut dairy-free yoghurt,
    to serve
maple syrup, for drizzling

Put the pears in a saucepan with the water – if there's not enough to just cover them, add some more. Add the sugar, orange zest and juice and spices.

Heat gently over a low to medium heat, stirring until the sugar dissolves, then increase the heat to high and bring to the boil. Reduce the heat to medium and simmer, covered, for 15 minutes, or until the pears are tender. Remove the pears with a slotted spoon and place them in a bowl. Discard the spices.

Increase the heat to high and heat until the poaching liquid starts to boil, then reduce the heat and add the dried fruit. Simmer for 5 minutes, or until reduced and syrupy.

Pour over the pears and set aside until cool. Cover and chill in the fridge overnight.

Alternatively, transfer to 6 glasses or serving bowls. Serve at room temperature with coconut yoghurt, drizzled with maple syrup.

VARIATIONS
· Serve with granola or muesli.
· Add some prunes, sultanas (golden raisins) and raisins.
· Stir in some blueberries, raspberries or blackberries.
· Use red wine instead of water for a mulled wine compôte.

INDEX

Page references in *italics* indicate images.